Let's Run!

Uncovering Faith and Finding Freedom

May God bless you
as you run your race
for Him! Lace up!
Jen

JENNIFER HAYES YATES

WESTBOW
PRESS®
A DIVISION OF THOMAS NELSON
& ZONDERVAN

Tessa Stanton (interior images) Kyle Hayes (author photo); Susan Chavis (cover image)

Scripture taken from the Holy Bible, NEW INTERNATIONAL VERSION®. Copyright © 1973, 1978, 1984 by Biblica, Inc. All rights reserved worldwide. Used by permission. NEW INTERNATIONAL VERSION® and NIV® are registered trademarks of Biblica, Inc. Use of either trademark for the offering of goods or services requires the prior written consent of Biblica US, Inc.

WestBow Press books may be ordered through booksellers or by contacting:

WestBow Press
A Division of Thomas Nelson & Zondervan
1663 Liberty Drive
Bloomington, IN 47403
www.westbowpress.com
1 (866) 928-1240

ISBN: 978-1-5127-0550-8 (sc)
ISBN: 978-1-5127-0551-5 (e)

Library of Congress Control Number: 2015912131

Print information available on the last page.

WestBow Press rev. date: 08/06/2015

Contents

Week 4– Faith and Ministry

Week 5– Faith and Opposition

Week 6– Faith and Victory

Introduction

Each year on January first, I ask God to give me a word in due season—a Scripture that is my verse for the year to meditate on, be challenged by, and focus on throughout the year. God always speaks and always confirms His Word to me in various ways, oftentimes even a little humorous.

The first year I did this, the Scripture was Matthew 6:33, and every time I looked at a digital clock, it would read 6:33. No kidding. All that year, God would constantly remind me to seek Him first every time I looked at a clock.

The following year, the verse was "It is finished!" That one scared me a little as I pondered what that meant for my life! Jesus showed up that year and ministered to me in amazing ways that included a small, hand-carved cross that a dear friend brought back to me from Israel. The cross was a simple reminder of those words Jesus spoke as He hung on a rugged cross—words that declare victory over sin and death. The title of our Easter musical that year was (Can you believe it?) "It Is Finished," again reminding me of the completed work of Christ on the cross. That year as I struggled with a recurrent sin, God reminded me that He died for my sin so that I could have victory over it. By the end of that year I was able to declare, "It is finished!"

The next year the verse was Matthew 7:7—"Ask and you will receive, seek and you will find, knock and the door will be opened." I wasn't even surprised when that Scripture, along with a picture of a beautiful door, was on the cover of my new monthly devotional. Our Sunday school book also featured a picture of an open door, and I felt God telling me He would open doors during that season. Towards the end of that year, our son answered God's call into full-time ministry, and God gently spoke that the open door was not for me, but for him.

Each day is an adventure with God, but I particularly look forward to the first of every year when I receive this special Word from God for my life's journey. So I was really distraught in 2014 when midnight came on January first and God was silent. I went to bed upset that God had not given me my "Word." Then the next morning, God began to speak an entire passage to my heart. I had to look it up, because I wasn't sure of every word, but I knew I was hearing His voice. The words He spoke were these from Hebrews 12:1-3:

> Therefore, since we are surrounded by such a great cloud of witnesses, let us
> throw off everything that hinders and the sin that so easily entangles, and let us

run with perseverance the race marked out for us. Let us fix our eyes on Jesus, the author and perfecter of our faith, who for the joy set before him endured the cross, scorning its shame, and sat down at the right hand of the throne of God. Consider him who endured such opposition from men, so that you will not grow weary and lose heart.

I felt God say in my spirit, "Let's run! It's time to lay everything else aside, look to Me, and run!" Just a couple of weeks later, a friend who had recently moved sent me a message about a women's conference at her new church, and she wanted me to come. Imagine my great excitement when I saw the theme of the conference. You guessed it! It was actually just the first two verses of Hebrews chapter 12, but I knew I had to be there. The conference was amazing, and I left hungry for more; thus I began to study this passage.

The book of Hebrews is intriguing and mysterious and decidedly Jewish—much more than I can begin to comprehend! We will look briefly at the background of the book and get an overall theme of each chapter and then study chapters 11 and 12 that focus on the passage God gave to me. Many of you are probably familiar with chapter 11 as the "Faith Hall of Fame." Because chapter 12 begins with the word *therefore*, we need to study what comes before, so this study focuses on the men and women of faith in chapter 11 and then the call to run the race in chapter 12.

We will have some background and then five daily readings for each week of the six-week study, followed by a weekend devotional that sums up the week's readings. If you are studying this book with a small group, I have included some notes at the end of each week for group discussion. Grab a study Bible, a hi-lighter, a pen, and let's see what God has in store.

Background on Hebrews

- Author: unknown (from AD 400-1600 assumed to be Paul, but many think that the language is different; the author doesn't identify himself as Paul usually does; Hebrews 2:3 suggests that the writer was not an eyewitness of Jesus but learned from one who was; some believe it may have been Barnabas or Apollos)
- Date: c. AD 64-68 (believed to be some time before AD 70; references to the temple are in present tense and the temple was destroyed in AD 70)
- Recipients: Jewish Christians (many references to Old Testament, the Law, Prophets, temple, and sacrificial system)
- Theme: supremacy and sufficiency of Christ as the mediator of God's grace
- Call to action: faith and perseverance

Overview of Chapters 1-10

- Chapter 1: The Son is superior to the angels who are "ministering spirits sent to serve those who will inherit salvation" (1:14).
- Chapter 2: We must pay attention to this message of the Gospel. The Law was spoken through angels, but salvation came through Christ. "...how shall we escape if we ignore such a great salvation?" (2:3).
- Chapter 3: Jesus is greater than Moses. Moses was a servant; Christ is the Son. Moses was faithful in God's house; Christ is over God's house.
- Chapter 4: There is a Sabbath-rest for those who believe. The Israelites that Moses led out of Egypt needed faith to enter the "rest" of the Promised Land, so we must have faith in the work of Christ to enter His spiritual and eternal "rest."
- Chapter 4-5: Jesus is our Great High Priest. Jesus' finished work on the cross gives us access to the Holy of Holies, the throne of God. We may come into God's presence through Christ and not a priest as in the Jewish tradition of sacrificial worship.
- Chapter 6: We have to mature in our understanding of Christ and His Word or we will face discipline. God cannot lie. He is our hope.
- Chapter 7: Jesus is greater than the priesthood because He lives forever. Melchizedek was a prefiguration of Christ or, as some believe, the pre-incarnate Christ Himself. Regardless, he was a priest and king in Genesis who set the stage for the Levitical priesthood. Jesus supersedes our need for a priest to offer sacrifices, because He became the sacrifice once for all.
- Chapter 8: Jesus is High Priest of a new covenant. The Jewish sacrificial system was a "copy and shadow of what is in heaven" (8:5). His covenant is superior and is "founded on better promises" (8:6).
- Chapter 9: The blood of Christ, the unblemished Lamb, is sufficient to cleanse from all sin.
- Chapter 10: We are made holy through Christ's sacrifice; therefore, we are to draw near to Him with faith, have our hearts cleansed, and live for Him with hope and perseverance.

Week 1

"Therefore, I urge you, brothers, in view of God's mercy,
to offer your bodies as living sacrifices, holy and pleasing
to God—this is your spiritual act of worship."

Romans 12:1

Faith and Worship

Day 1—A Sure Hope

When I was growing up, my parents were runners. Back in the '70s, when Dr. Robert Atkins first came out with the low-carbohydrate diet, Mama and Daddy began eating low-carb and running. They would train every other night with my uncle and then run in 10k races, which are 6.2 miles. What I mostly remember is going to the different 10k events with them. They ran with my uncle, so my sister and I would usually be on the sidelines with our aunt.

I remember shivering and sipping hot chocolate while we waited for a race to be over. I can recall being at the finish line, straining to see around the people taller than I. I just wanted to get a glimpse of my mama and daddy as they finished the race. I saw how tired and sweaty many of the runners were. Some people would collapse from exertion. I wanted to see my parents, give them some water, and know that they were okay.

As soon as I laid eyes on them, I would begin to shout, "Come on! You can do it! You've got this! Run! Run! Run!" I wanted to encourage them all the way. I would run along the sideline for the last few yards until they crossed the line. And, man, was I proud of them when they did. They had endured to the end.

As we begin to study the heroes of faith in Hebrews chapter 11, I can almost see Abraham, Moses, Sarah, and many others all crowded around the finish line. They're calling out to us, "Come on! You can do it! Don't give up! Run!" They just want us to endure to the end.

So, come along with me as we study the lives of these men and women of faith. Let's learn what faith looks like and why it's necessary to run our race.

NIV Read Hebrews 11:1 and copy it here. Now faith is the confidence of things hoped for and the assurance about what we do not see.

Tell in your own words what that means to you.

Notice that faith is trust in the unseen, not the unknown. Study the following synonyms for the word *faith*: assurance, confirmation, proof, evidence, conviction.

Where does one get proof of something unseen? (Hint: not unknown!)

Let's look at 11:2. Read it in your Bible and answer the following:

Who are the ancients?

Why were they commended?

Read Habakkuk 2:4 and copy it here.

If they were commended for living by faith, which is being sure of what we hope for, what do you think these ancients were hoping for?

Look up the following Scriptures and jot a note about each one:
- Job 13:15
- Psalm 119:74
- Psalm 130:7-8
- Isaiah 40:31
- Lamentations 3:21-23

Read Hebrews 11:3. How does this verse relate to verse 1? What words do they have in common?

If we believe that God created the visible universe at His command, but we didn't see it, that is faith. Being certain of what you hope for is faith. The ancients were hoping for salvation; what are you hoping for—in your personal life, your marriage, your family, your church, your career? Take a few moments to think about this and journal your thoughts.

Day 2—A Genuine Heart

What do you think the relationship is between faith and worship? Today's lesson is about genuine worship from the heart. King David once went to Araunah the Jebusite to purchase his threshing floor so that he might build an altar to the Lord. Araunah tried to give it to David for free, but David responded, "I will not take for the Lord what is yours, or sacrifice a burnt offering that costs me nothing" (1 Chronicles 21:24b). David wanted his worship to cost him something. What about you and me? Does our worship cost us anything? Let's travel in history all the way back to the beginning, to Adam and Eve's children. Let's see how faith and worship go hand-in-hand.

Read Hebrews 11:4 in your Bible. Now turn to Genesis and read 4:1-8.

What was Abel's occupation?

What was Cain's occupation?

Read Genesis chapters 1-3. Do you see any mention of God requiring an offering?

What do you think motivated Cain and Abel to give offerings to God?

What was the difference between the two offerings? Write below what the Bible says about each offering.

Cain's offering:

Abel's offering:

Many scholars have speculated on why God did not accept Cain's offerings. Some suggest that Cain offered God the fruit of the ground that God had cursed in Genesis 3:17-19. Therefore, it was not acceptable.

What stands out to me is the word *firstborn* applied to Abel's offering from his flock. The Scripture does not refer to Cain's offering as being *firstfruits*.

Read Hebrews 11:4 again. Why does Scripture say Abel was commended?

What do you believe to be the purpose of the offering?

Do you believe it was intended as an act of worship? If that is the case, let's look at the difference between offering "some of the fruits of the soil" and "some of the firstborn of his flock."

In Exodus 23:19, the Israelites were commanded to bring the firstfruits of their soil to the house of God as an offering. The *NIV Study Bible* note reads "The offering of firstfruits was an acknowledgment that the harvest was from the Lord and belonged wholly to him."[1]

The Layman's Bible Encyclopedia states, "In the Old Testament the firstborn male, whether of human beings or animals, was regarded as belonging to the Lord. Firstborn animals were usually sacrificed; firstborn sons were usually dedicated to the service of the Lord."[2]

The offering was an act of worship. One son offered his best to God, knowing that everything he had came from God. One offered worship that was not from the heart. It lacked faith, a genuine spirit, and the acknowledgment that it all came from his Lord. His heart just wasn't in his worship. God is pleased with and honors our worship when it comes from the heart, when it's genuine, when it's faith-filled.

In other words, when we offer our best to him—the best of our time, our service, our tithe, our worship—we show God that by faith we believe all we have comes from Him. God is not looking for us to show up at church and sign in or punch a clock as if we are just doing our duty. Our worship, our quiet time with Him, and our service should flow out of a personal relationship with God.

We shouldn't come to God and give to Him out of obligation or even just discipline. I believe that's what Cain did. We see from his response to God's approval of his brother's offering that Cain's heart was not right with God. He still brought an offering, but God saw his heart. God won't bless our *faithless* acts of worship. He blesses a soul that delights in Him and loves Him and gives to Him out of that devotion and love. When we've spent time as His feet and talked with Him and listened to His voice, when we've tasted and seen that He is good, and then come with our acts of worship—our spiritual offering—it will come from a genuine heart that loves God. That's the heart God delights in.

Think about your worship. Are you just going through the motions? Or are you offering God your best out of gratitude for all that He has given you? Journal a few sentences about your attitude toward worship.

Day 3—A Faithful Walk

Many years ago, I went to a "gospel singing." If you live in the South, you understand what I'm talking about! Before the singing started, the members of the group were at a table in the lobby, selling CDs and talking with people. I was at the table looking at the merchandise, when an older gentleman in the group walked over and started talking to me. I can't explain to you what happened next, except that I was suddenly in tears and couldn't swallow for the lump in my throat. I couldn't even speak to him. He had so much of God's holiness in him that I was overcome with the sweetness of God's Spirit. I don't know if you've ever met anyone like that before, but this was a man who clearly didn't just profess faith in Christ; he walked with God. He didn't just sing about Jesus; he knew the One of whom he sang. That's how I picture Enoch, a man who carried the very presence of God on his life.

Read Hebrews 11:5-6. Fill in the blank. "By _____ Enoch was taken from this life, so that he did not experience death…"

Read Genesis 5:21-24. Now go back and skim the genealogy in Genesis 5:1-20. What do you notice that is similar about all the genealogies listed?

Did you notice what I did? They each give an account of a man who lived a certain number of years, became a father, had other children, lived a certain total number of years, and then died.

What is different about the account of Enoch's life?

The genealogy is given right after an account of Cain's descendants and the birth of Seth, another son of Adam and Eve. Cain's descendants followed in his evil path of sin and murder.

Read Genesis 4:23-24. Lamech was seventh in line from Adam through Cain. Enoch was seventh in line from Adam through Seth. (Cain also had a son named Enoch, but he is not the same Enoch we read about in verses 5-6.)

The genealogy seems to be pointing out two important truths:

Even though the life spans seem incredibly long, *they all died*, which is evidence of God's truth that if Adam and Eve ate of the Tree of the Knowledge of Good and Evil, they would die. From that point on, man needed a Savior.

The curse of sin and death was repeated generation after generation, so apparently the fathers were not raising their sons to follow God. But after we read of Seth's birth and his becoming a father in 4:26, the Bible says that "at that time men began to call on the Lord."

I think there are some really important lessons here. Look again at Genesis 5:21-22. When did Enoch begin to walk with God?

Do you think that maybe becoming a father made Enoch get serious about his relationship with the Lord?

The Amplified Bible says that Enoch "walked with God [in habitual fellowship]."

What do you believe that it means to walk with God "in habitual fellowship"?

What is the difference between walking with God and just living?

How many times does the passage say that Enoch walked with God?

Read Hebrews 11:5 again. Why was Enoch commended?

Enoch is one of only two men that the Bible tells us did not experience death but were simply taken to God (the other was Elijah). What does this tell you about the life God takes pleasure in?

Abel was commended as a righteous man, and Enoch was commended as one who pleased God; the writer of Hebrews describes them both as men who lived by faith. Read Hebrews 11:6. Why is it impossible to please God without faith?

According to this verse, faith requires more than just belief; it requires seeking Him. Enoch didn't just believe that God exists, but he had faith that if he sought the Lord, he would find Him. He believed He could walk with God, and he did.

How about you? Do you walk with God in habitual fellowship daily?

If not, how could you make daily time with God a habit?

What steps could you take to be closer to God?

How would that affect your worship?

Day 4—A Holy Fear

When I first graduated from college, I began teaching at a Christian school. Coming from a broken home, I really didn't know anything about raising a Christian family, but I had the opportunity to work with and be around others who did. I learned as much about family worship at that school as I did about teaching.

I learned that the husband/father is the head of the home and should lead his family. I learned that children need to be trained in the things of God from a young age and that it is our responsibility as parents to instruct them. I learned to have family prayer and Bible reading, to teach my children to pray and love God's Word, to teach them biblical principles and discipline them with lots of love and grace.

I will forever be grateful for the staff at Jesus Is Lord Christian School for being such godly examples to me when I was young and just beginning to start a family. Noah, too, understood the relationship between faith and the family altar. He obeyed the Word of the Lord, and because he did, his whole family was saved.

Read Hebrews 11:7 and copy it below.

We have a good bit of reading to do today. We will start in Genesis 5:25-32. (Notice that Methuselah had a son named Lamech, but he is not the same Lamech we looked at yesterday who was a descendant of Cain. This is the lineage from Seth. This Lamech was the father of Noah.)

Now let's look at Noah's story. Read Genesis 6:1-22. The first part of chapter 6 describes the intermarriage of two parties: "the sons of God" and "the daughters of men." Scholars have interpreted this passage in different ways. The Hebrew that is translated "sons of God" could refer to angels as it does in other places, such as Job, and would therefore mean that angels actually came and married women on earth. Other scholars say this is not possible, and that "sons of God" refers to godly men and "daughters of men" to ungodly women. This would make sense following the passage describing the godly descendants of Seth as opposed to the ungodly descendants of Cain.[3]

The next few verses refer to the Nephilim, a Hebrew word meaning "fallen ones." These were a large and strong race who were considered heroes, probably in battle. The reference to fallen ones means that they were considered wicked.

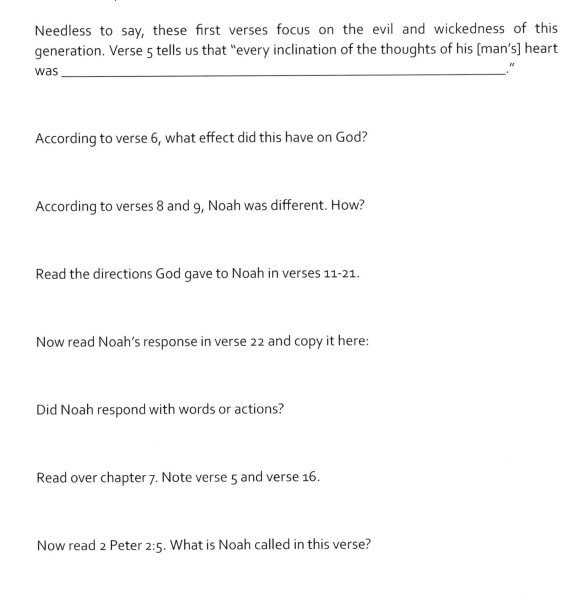

Needless to say, these first verses focus on the evil and wickedness of this generation. Verse 5 tells us that "every inclination of the thoughts of his [man's] heart was _____."

According to verse 6, what effect did this have on God?

According to verses 8 and 9, Noah was different. How?

Read the directions God gave to Noah in verses 11-21.

Now read Noah's response in verse 22 and copy it here:

Did Noah respond with words or actions?

Read over chapter 7. Note verse 5 and verse 16.

Now read 2 Peter 2:5. What is Noah called in this verse?

Apparently during the 120 years that it took Noah to build the ark, he was preaching to his contemporaries, urging them to repent before the coming judgment. His wife and his sons and their wives were the only ones to escape the judgment.

Let's go back to Hebrews and read 11:7 again. Noah obeyed God when he was warned about things "not yet seen." What was not yet seen?

Noah lived in a "landlocked" region where it would have seemed impossible for there to be enough water to float a huge boat!

The Bible says Noah built the ark out of "holy fear." What do you think that means?

The second part of this verse tells us that "by his _____ he condemned the world and became heir of the righteousness that comes by faith." In what way did Noah "condemn the world"?

Noah was able to trust completely, even in things "not yet seen" when others did not. In so doing, his faith was justified, and their unbelief was judged. It is a story of both judgment and redemption, in that God redeems those who believe and act on that belief.

Read Genesis 8:20-21. What did Noah do when he and his family came out of the ark?

"…every inclination of the thoughts of his heart was only evil all the time." Except for one man. One man whose holy fear of the Almighty led him to a place of shelter and refuge in a boat—a preacher of righteousness who built an altar and worshiped God.

As we run our race for Christ, we may not always see clearly or understand what God is calling us to do. We may sometimes be called to obey when it doesn't make sense or goes against what everyone else is doing. But by faith, we can enter a place of refuge from the storm of sin and temptation all around. We can live a life that preaches righteousness to those around us and warns them of the judgment to come. And we can certainly build a family altar and lead our family to worship the one true God. Oh, that we each might live with that holy fear. And may the Lord smell the pleasing aroma of our worship.

Day 5—A Sacred Trust

I can still remember the first time I witnessed true worship. I didn't grow up in a Christian home, but I had been to church some off and on. When I graduated from high school, I started dating a guy whose mother was a believer. She made him go to church as long as he lived at home. Needless to say, I sometimes found myself there as well—not because I wanted to go to church, but that was the only way I would see my boyfriend.

I remember one night in particular that the preacher's daughter was singing. I don't remember the song, but I remember her worship. I remember the look on her face as she sang and the lifting of her hands as she worshiped. And I wanted whatever it was that she had. Because I knew it was something I needed. I knew in that moment that I was lost.

Have you ever thought of worship as a witness? Let's follow Abram in his pursuit of God and see how he worshiped God everywhere he went.

Romans 4:11 calls Abraham "the father of all who believe." He is mentioned in the Hebrews "Hall of Faith" in twelve different verses! We will only study three of these verses today.

> Read Hebrew 11:8-10. Now turn to Genesis and let's start in 11:27 and read through 12:9. Where were Abram and his family from?

> Where was his father, Terah, taking the family?

> Where did they settle instead?

Ur was the capital of Sumer, a bustling city of commerce, whose people worshiped the moon-god, Sin. Ironic name for a false god, huh? Haran was another important city in Mesopotamia, considered "one of the chief centers for the worship of Sin."[4] Both of these cities had been home to Abram. Can you picture these ancient cities with their false gods and idol worship?

Read Genesis 12:1 in *The Amplified Bible*:

Now [in Haran] the Lord said to Abram, Go for yourself [for your own advantage] away from your country, from your relatives and your father's house, to the land that I will show you.

Why did God say for Abram to go away?

Turn to Joshua 24:2. Abram's father, Terah, was an idolater, meaning that he worshiped idols or false gods. God was calling Abram to separate himself from everything that he knew—his home, his family, and his friends—because he lived among a people, including his own father, who worshiped other gods. God was calling him out from among them for his own good.

Look at Genesis 12:1 again. Did God tell Abram where he was going?

God gave Abram only one step: go. Abram had to take the first step before God would show him the next step. But what did God promise Abram if he would obey? Read Genesis 12:2-3.

List everything God promised Abram:
1.
2.
3.
4.
5.
6.
7.

Genesis 12:4 says "So Abram left, as the Lord had told him." Here again we see, like Noah, a prompt obedience without knowledge of what was to come. Why do you think Abram was able to leave everything he knew to go somewhere he didn't know?

Look at verse 7. Fill in the blank: So he built an altar there to the Lord,
_____

Abram worshiped the God who had appeared to him. Again we see that faith is not blind. Abram followed One whom he knew. Perhaps Abram had witnessed the idolatry of his father and the wickedness of his culture and knew that his God was calling him to something better.

Many times God calls us to separate ourselves "for our own advantage." He may call us out of a situation or a circle of influence because He knows what is harmful to us and what is good for us. We may not see the path ahead, but we can follow the footsteps of our Lord, one step at a time.

Now go back to Hebrews 11:9-10. Abram spent a lot of time in tents, journeying to a place he couldn't name, and settled as a foreigner in a strange land. It wasn't easy, I'm sure. Maybe God has you in a strange place right now. It may even be an unfamiliar or uncomfortable place. Like Abram, you can place a sacred trust in your God and know that He is working for "your own advantage." Because, ultimately, the city Abram was looking for was not a temporary dwelling, but a permanent home in the land paved with streets of gold. Ecclesiastes 3:11 says that God has set eternity in the hearts of men. Abram was looking ahead.

Has God called you out of something familiar and led you to a new place, maybe even an uncomfortable place? Remember the testimony of Abram and just worship the Lord for who He is no matter where you are.

Weekend Devo Faith and Worship

Today, I want you to sit and rest in God's presence. Get your coffee and a cozy spot and relax—no studying—just reading and meditating on God's truth.

Now that we have looked at the first few verses of Hebrews chapter 11, let's recap what we have learned.

1. Faith is putting our complete hope, belief, and trust in God, regardless of what we see with our own eyes.
2. Abel brought God an offering by faith, from his heart, as an act of worship.
3. Enoch walked with God by faith in habitual fellowship and worship.
4. Noah believed God by faith, obeyed Him, and led his family to salvation and worship.
5. Abram left everything by faith to follow God, and he built an altar of worship everywhere he went.

What does this mean for our lives? I think we can make five important applications to our own faith and worship.

First, faith is necessary for salvation.

"For it is by grace you have been saved, *through faith*, and this not from yourselves, it is the gift of God—not by works, so that no one can boast" (Ephesians 2:8-9, emphasis added).

"I have been crucified with Christ and I no longer live, but Christ lives in me. The life I live in the body, *I live by faith* in the Son of God, who loved me and gave himself for me" (Galatians 2:20, emphasis added).

We have to be certain of what we believe about the life, death, burial, and resurrection of Jesus Christ in order to come to Him and be saved.

> Application: Do you believe in Jesus Christ as your Savior and Lord? If you have never surrendered your life to God by faith, please turn to the back of this book and read how to become a follower of the Lord Jesus Christ on the page titled "New Life."

Second, faith will lead us to worship, which is our deepest need as humans. We all have a desire to worship something. Faith in Jesus Christ will draw us to His feet in true, heartfelt worship, as it did for Abel. True worship will cost us something.

> Application: Do you come into God's house with your heart ready to worship? This Sunday, begin your morning by pre-prayer-ing for worship. Ask God to cleanse you of

any sin, free your mind from any distractions, and put a spirit of worship in your heart. Pray for the teachers, worship leaders, and pastor for God's anointing on them as they serve. Ask God to fill your sanctuary with praise and to let your heart be fertile soil to receive the seed of His Word.

Third, faith will lead us not only to outward worship, but to a lifestyle of worship.

"Therefore, I urge you, brothers, in view of God's mercy, to offer your bodies as living sacrifices, holy and pleasing to God—this is your *spiritual act of worship*" (Romans 12:1, emphasis added).

> Application: Do you have a daily quiet time with the Lord? I know this is difficult to achieve consistently in our busy world today, but I believe it is essential to a lifestyle of worship as we saw in the life of Enoch, who walked with God. Commit today to begin every day with God. Set your alarm clock 15 minutes earlier than normal and plan a spot to meet with Him for prayer and devotion. You will not regret it!

Fourth, faith will affect our family time. If we truly believe by faith that God is who He says He is, this belief will impact our family structure. Noah's faith affected his entire family.

> Application: If you are married and/or have children, plan family dinner time around the table as many nights of the week as possible. Do not allow technology or negative comments for your family dinner time. Talk with your family, read a Scripture, and pray together. If you live alone, plan at least one night a week to turn off the television, light a candle, and enjoy a meal in fellowship with the Lord. You may also want to invite someone to share a meal with you in your home once a week.

Fifth, if we truly believe, our faith will affect those around us. Abraham's faith led him to worship everywhere he went as he followed God. We, too, can let our worship be a witness.

> Application: Leave your mark for Jesus everywhere you go this week! At the grocery store, post office, or in your workplace, be the person who shines brightest! Share a smile, encouragement, joy in the midst of uncertain times—so that others will see something different about you. Let your lifestyle of worship be a witness to the world.

Friend, don't feel that you have to apply every one of these suggestions, but find something in today's time together that speaks to your heart; then get up and get out there and let your faith lead you to worship the only One who is worthy!

Small Group Ideas

If you are meeting weekly with a small group, you may want to incorporate some of the ideas we used at my church when we did this study.

- We drew names and committed to pray for the other person for the entire six weeks of the study.
- We made bracelets by braiding three strands of colorful hemp cord and then tied them on the arm of the person whose name we drew as a reminder that we were praying for them. The three strands represent us, the other person, and the Holy Spirit, who intercedes for us. Use the following Scriptures: Ecclesiastes 4:12, Romans 8:26.
- Use these questions for discussion:
  - What spoke to your heart most from this week's study?
  - What does faith look like in our world today?
  - What is the difference between outward religious activity and true worship from the heart?
  - What does it mean to "walk with the Lord"?
  - What is holy fear?
  - How does your family worship together at home?
  - How can our worship be a witness?
  - Share your faith story/testimony.
  - Which application did you commit to put into practice this week?

- Depending on the size of your group, you may discuss together or break into smaller groups.
- If time is limited, you could print the questions on index cards and draw a few out to discuss.

Week 2

"The unfolding of your words gives light; it gives understanding to the simple"
Psalm 119:130

Faith and the Word

Day 1—A Precious Promise

I don't know about you, but I get it wrong. A lot. Sometimes in my impatience to see God move in my life, I tend to help Him out a little. Take this Bible study, for instance. When I received the provision to have it published, I got really excited because I had heard from the Lord! I knew that I was supposed to get the book published. So I sent it off to a self-publishing company and waited for them to do the theological review. Then I had lots of ideas that I thought would make the study better.

As soon as the manuscript passed theological review, I emailed the publisher with some of the changes I wanted to make—the weekend devos and small group ideas. The publisher then informed me that since the manuscript passed their theological review, no changes could be made. I was devastated. I knew the book was not what God wanted it to be, but I had not waited on Him to lead me. I believed His Word to me, but I wanted it accomplished in my time, not His.

Has that ever happened to you? It happened to Sarah.

Today we will read Hebrews 11:11-12, but from the *KJV*. The *NIV* renders the translation as "By faith *Abraham*..." but with a text note that reads "or 'by faith even *Sarah* '"[5] (emphasis added). The *KJV* reads:

> Through faith also Sarah herself received strength to conceive seed, and was delivered of a child when she was past age, because she judged him faithful who had promised. Therefore sprang there even of one, and him as good as dead, so many as the stars of the sky in multitude, and as the sand which is by the sea shore innumerable.

The Amplified Bible renders the translation this way:

> Because of faith also Sarah herself received physical power to conceive a child, even when she was long past the age for it, because she considered [God] who had given her the promise to be reliable and trustworthy and true to His word. So from one man, though he was physically as good as dead, there have sprung

descendants whose number is as the stars of heaven and as countless as the innumerable sands on the seashore.

I believe these passages focus on the faith of Sarah. I love this, because she was *so* not perfect! Let's go back and look at her story in Genesis. We already learned from Genesis 11:30 that Sarai (Sarah) was barren. In Jewish culture, this would have been disgraceful, but it is also a reminder that the Jewish nation came through the power of God and not natural means.

Skim Genesis chapters 12-14. Now read chapters 15-16.

What did God promise Abraham?

Why did Abraham question this promise (see Genesis 15:1-3)?

What was Sarai's solution to the problem (chapter 16)?

Read 16:3. How long had they been in Canaan?

Some time had passed since the promise, so Sarai was taking matters into her own hands. It was an ancient Assyrian custom if a woman were barren, for the maidservant to attempt to provide the male heir for the man. It wasn't a godly custom, but it wasn't unheard of!

What do you think made Sarai suggest this to Abram?

Do you think she thought she was helping God carry out the promise, or do you think she got tired of waiting for the promise?

Why do you think her maidservant, Hagar, began to despise her?

Had Sarai helped or hindered the situation?

Read 17:1-18:15. God confirmed His covenant from chapter 15. How old was Abram at the time of this?

What were the conditions of the covenant? (See 17:1.)

God confirmed His promise to Abraham but let him know that he must walk in obedience to receive the promise. What did God tell them to name the son that was to come?

Isaac means "laughter." In chapter 18, what was Sarah's response to the Lord's promise to Abraham of a son from his own body?

If Sarah took matters in her own hands with Hagar, mistreated her, and then laughed when God said she would have a child when she was way past childbearing years, why did God say in Hebrews 11 that she had faith?

I believe Sarah is in the Hall of Faith simply because she considered God faithful to His promise. Whether she thought she needed to help with the plan (Hagar) or whether she laughed in awe of a God who could make an old woman conceive, Sarah knew God keeps His promises. She heard God talk to Abraham. They had followed God from Haran into Canaan. She had witnessed the faithfulness of God. And with or without her help, the God she believed in would come through.

God's plans for Abraham and Sarah were not thwarted by their mistakes! God had a plan to make them the parents of an entire nation that He would set apart to worship Him. He chose them because He saw their hearts. Hear me clearly! They were not chosen because they were perfect. They were chosen because God believed that they would "direct [their] children and their household after [them] to keep the way of the Lord by doing what is right and just..." (Hebrews 18:19). And Sarah's impatience with God's timing didn't stop God from fulfilling His promise.

In fact, read Hebrews 11:11-12 again. Sarah considered Him faithful who made the promise. Bottom line. Her impatience caused some problems and consequences, for sure. The Jews are the descendants of Isaac; the Arabs are the descendants of Ishmael. These two groups have lived in conflict ever since. But the promise (Jesus) was fulfilled through the promised son. God is true to His Word. He doesn't make promises and then break them.

And He doesn't take our mistakes and throw them aside. Read again Genesis 16:7-16; 17:18-19; and 17:23-26. God had not forgotten Hagar or Ishmael. God uses all things, even our mistakes, for our good and for His glory. Read Genesis 21:1-21. God was with both boys because they were sons of Abraham, and God made him a promise. A very precious promise. A promise that one day led to the birth of another precious Son, who would redeem all our mistakes.

Remember the mistake I made with the Bible study? God knew my heart, and as I prayed every day for weeks that God would redeem my mistake, guess what happened? For some reason, that publisher closed their doors and returned my manuscript. I was able to make the changes I felt God wanted and then submit the manuscript to another publisher. We will make mistakes. We will get tired and impatient. But if we truly believe that God is who He says He is and that His promises are true, then God will see our hearts and redeem our mistakes. He will still use us and receive us into His eternal Kingdom. May we consider Him faithful who has made the promise.

Day 2—A Better Country

The Christian school where I teach high school is very small. We plan a junior-senior trip every other year because the two classes can be combined. This little group of juniors and seniors spends an entire year planning fund raisers, working, selling, and dreaming about the spring break trip to Williamsburg, Virginia. We visit Colonial Williamsburg, Jamestown, and Yorktown; but, of course, the most-awaited destination is Busch Gardens.

Few activities excite the minds of young people quite like the thrill of roller coasters, rides, shows, and food! Did I mention how much *I* love Busch Gardens? We always go there the first day of our trip, because we can't contain our excitement any longer.

So, on this last trip, we planned and worked and sold all year long—doughnuts, Christmas ornaments, 2-year planners, hot dogs, pancakes... We booked the trip through the hotel, which included our accommodations and tickets to each park. When we arrived on the first day, it was nearly evening, so we went out to eat and planned for our first day at Busch Gardens. The next morning I went to the desk to get our tickets and was told to pick up our hopper passes at Colonial Williamsburg.

So off we went, so excited for the day that lay ahead. We stopped by Colonial Williamsburg, and I went in to get everyone's passes. As I was checking out, the lady said, "You do know that Busch Gardens is closed until Friday, right?" We were leaving on Thursday.

I couldn't speak. I can't even tell you what I felt. I thought, "Surely, there's been some kind of mistake. Wouldn't the hotel that booked our trip six months ago know that they sold us passes for this date?" But, no, they were very sorry. Must have overlooked that. Nothing they could do.

Have you ever hoped and dreamed for something, only to find that it was never going to happen in this life?

> Read Hebrews 11:13-16. Scholars agree that "all these people" refers to Abraham, Sarah, Isaac, and Jacob, (the descendants referred to at the end of verse 12). So then why does the Scripture say they did *not* receive the promise?

> Read Genesis 12:2-3 again. Let's review the promises to Abraham.
> 1. I will make you a great nation.
> 2. I will bless you.
> 3. I will make your name great.
> 4. You will be a blessing.
> 5. I will bless those who bless you.
> 6. I will curse those who curse you.
> 7. All people on earth will be blessed through you.

God told Abraham in Genesis 15:7 that He would give him the Promised Land, but in verses 15-16 that Abraham would go to his fathers in peace, and his descendants would come back and possess the land. In chapter 17, God renewed the covenant with Abraham and told him in verse 8 that he was living now as an alien in the land, but that his descendants would possess that land and that He would be their God.

> So what part of these promises did Abraham receive (see Hebrews 11:17b)?

He received the promised child, Isaac. But Abraham never received the fulfillment of the promise, which was Jesus (the ultimate Seed who would bring blessing to all the earth through the gift of salvation) and possession of the Promised Land (which God had already told him he would not personally receive, but his descendants would).

Abraham and Sarah "saw" the promise, because that is what faith is—belief in what is physically not seen, but "seen" by faith. They hoped and believed in something better—a heavenly home, the permanent "rest" of Canaan. Abraham said in Genesis 23:4 to the Hittites, "I am a stranger and sojourner with you."

Abraham lived as a stranger in this world, because He believed God's promise of an ultimate Promised Land where he would find rest. He believed that through his seed, all the earth would be blessed. In John 8:56 Jesus said, "Your father Abraham rejoiced at the thought of seeing my day; he saw it and was glad."

Abraham, Sarah, Isaac, Jacob—all were living by faith when they died, not having yet received the Promise, because Christ had not yet come. But they welcomed that Promise from a distance, knowing that when Christ did come and die for the sins of the world—past, present, and future—that they would receive the Promise. That is why the Bible says that God is not ashamed to be called their God, for He has prepared a city for them.

How about you? Are you living for now, settling in, getting comfortable with life on earth? Hanging pictures on the walls as if you are here to stay? Short-sighted faith will struggle with pain. This world is fallen, broken, and temporary. When the pain and disappointments come, we need to be able to pack up and move on, like a sojourner just passing through.

Don't long for the country you have left behind—the sin, temptations, and pleasures of the world. And don't settle in for a comfortable country now; it is always changing, never satisfying, shifting sand. Like Abraham and Sarah, let your heart long for a better country—the one God has prepared for you. He is not ashamed to be called your God.

Abraham and Sarah welcomed salvation from a distance. How much more should we (who have salvation) walk by faith, with our hearts set on our eternal home—a far better country.

Day 3—A Proven Faith

As a teacher, I give lots of tests. The purpose of testing is to assess what a student has learned and, consequently, what he has not learned. Testing helps me to understand, not only what a student is not learning, but also what I may not be effectively teaching. The greatest aspect of testing, however, is that if a student doesn't pass a test, he will usually get another chance.

You see, our testing is cumulative; that is, we test at three weeks, six weeks, and then again at nine weeks. The nine week test will cover all of the information I have taught in those nine weeks. So each student has an opportunity to see a lot of the same information again. With a little extra effort, he will usually pass it the second time.

Testing is not usually enjoyed by students, but it is necessary to confirm that the educational process is working and to prove to teachers that their goals are being met. Likewise, we don't normally enjoy the tests we face in life, but they are sometimes necessary.

Abraham faced a test that makes us want to look away. But we can't. God wants us to see it.

Let's begin our lesson today by reading Hebrews 11:17-19. Of course, our next step is to read this account of Abraham and Isaac from Genesis 22:1-18. The Scripture says "some time later." We don't actually know how old Isaac was at this time. But we do know this: he *was* the promised son!

Both passages tell us that God tested Abraham. Let's not confuse test with tempt. James 1:13 tells us that God does not tempt us. But God will test us to confirm our faith in Him or to prove our commitment to Him. The testing is to reveal what is within us. Read Exodus 20:20 and Deuteronomy 8:2.

> Now please read Hebrews 11:17, Genesis 22:2, and Genesis 22:16. What do they all have in common?

Did somebody forget Ishmael? Technically, Isaac was not Abraham's *only* son, but he *was* the only son of the promise. Recall John 3:16. God gave His one and only Son. We will see much prophecy of Jesus in these Scriptures.

God had asked Abraham to sacrifice the one thing that meant more to him than anything in the world. The promise. The son. The miracle that came to him only through the power of God and not by natural means. The one thing that all the promise of the future depended on! There would be no nation without Isaac. There would be no descendants as numerous as the stars! He was called to sacrifice the means by which all men would one day be saved!

> Please read Hebrews 11:18, Genesis 21:12, and Romans 9:6-8.

The NIV uses the term "reckoned." It means to be counted or to settle an account. It is through Isaac that the promise was settled and the descendants counted. So Abraham reasoned that if God could provide the son, then He could provide the sacrifice. What a beautiful prophetic picture of our Lord!

> Genesis 22:3 reads "early the next morning." Abraham didn't debate and discuss and talk it over with Sarah and "pray about it" for a week. He just got up and saddled his donkey and took Isaac on a trip. Read verse 5. Who did Abraham tell his servants would come back after the sacrifice was made?

He said we will worship and then we will come back to you. Not *I* will come back to you, but *we* will come back to you.

When Isaac asked his father where the offering was, Abraham told him God would provide the lamb. Abraham had no doubt that the God who provided the son would provide the sacrifice. Even if it meant he had to kill Isaac and that God would raise him from the dead (Hebrews 11:19).

> What can we learn from Abraham's example of faith?

The immediate fulfillment of God providing the sacrifice was in the ram that was caught in the thicket, but the ultimate fulfillment was in the sacrifice of the spotless Lamb of God, our Lord Jesus Christ, the one and only Son of the Father!

Like Abraham, we will be tested. Like Abraham, we get to choose how we will respond. Abraham responded with faith.

1. Prompt obedience (Early the next morning, he got up.)
2. Worship (We will worship and then we will come back to you.)
3. Trust in God (God himself will provide the lamb.)
4. Action (Then he reached out his hand and took the knife to slay his son.)

Read James 2:17-24. Faith without works is dead. Abraham didn't just believe God would come through. He went all the way with his obedience and trusted God with the outcome. That's real faith. When we are willing to lay our "Isaac"—that holy, beloved thing—on the altar of sacrifice, knowing that God will provide the lamb.

I don't know Abraham's heart. Maybe he needed to let go a little. God surely tested him for a reason. But I do know this: Abraham passed his test. May the same be said of you and me.

Day 4—A Future Blessing

I was a young Christian when I became a wife and started a family. God was so faithful to surround me with mentors who challenged me, encouraged me, and taught me the ways of God. One of the first things I learned was through a book that our pastor recommended when we got married. It's called *Giving the Blessing*[6] by Gary Smalley and John Trent. In this book, I learned the importance of speaking blessings over our family.

In Jewish culture, the blessing was spoken by the father over the children and carried significant weight, as we will study today. For our family, we learned the importance of speaking words of encouragement and honor, validation and affirmation. The blessing may include actual prayers or Scriptures that we pray over our children or our spouse.

Blessing is the opposite of cursing. Satan may intend curses for us, but God's will for us is to be blessed. We can reverse the curse of Satan, because there is power in God's Word. Isaac knew that. Even though he was deceived and betrayed, he spoke the blessing over his sons and trusted God with the results.

Today's lesson is only one verse. Let's read Hebrews 11:20. Write it below:

To understand today's verse, we must read over several chapters of Genesis. Skim each chapter quickly and summarize it here:

Chapter 23:
Why was it important to Abraham that Sarah be buried in Canaan?

Chapter 24:
Why was it important to Abraham to get Isaac a wife from his own people and not the Canaanites?

Chapter 25:
What prophecy did the Lord give to Rebekah about the twins in her womb?

What were their names?

Which was the firstborn?

In ancient culture, the law of primogeniture stated that the firstborn son would receive at least a double share of his father's property at the father's death.[7] The younger son would be subservient to the older.[8] But from the Lord's prophecy, we already see that this natural order would change.

Because Esau traded his birthright for a bowl of stew, he gave up, not only the inheritance of Isaac, but also the covenant promise of Abraham and Isaac. Yes, Jacob was a deceiver; but Esau proved that he was not very concerned with the covenant or its promises. Continue to skim.

Chapter 26:1-6:

Chapter 27:
What did Rebekah and Jacob trick Isaac into doing at his deathbed?

The blessing on one's deathbed was an oral statement that was legally binding in ancient culture. [9] Esau had already given up his birthright, and then Jacob tricked him out of his father's blessing as well.

What was the blessing given to Jacob?

What was the blessing given to Esau?

Chapter 28:1-5:
Why do you think it was important to Isaac that Jacob marry someone from their own family and take possession of the land they lived in?

Isaac is in the Hall of Faith because he believed that his descendants would inherit the promise God gave to Abraham. He made choices as a father based on that belief. The tradition of blessing children was an ancient practice that meant the father was speaking words of divine care, encouragement, honor, and future grace. Isaac didn't choose Jacob to receive the blessing and, therefore, inherit the promise. But only one child could be the line through which the promise came.

Esau gave up his right to the covenant promises, so Jacob inherited them. Jacob's name means "deceiver." But as we will see in the next lesson, God changed all of that. Because Jacob received the blessing. And the blessing of God changes everything.

Day 5—A Chosen Blessing

My mom is known by everyone as Mema. She acquired this name when she first became a grandmother, and she's been known by this name ever since. She takes seriously her call to be a "mema." She loves her grandchildren and has probably instilled as much into them as their own parents have.

Mema knows how to give the blessing: looking her grandkids in the eye as they talk to her, valuing them as people, validating her love and affection to each one, spending quality time with them, and, of course, lots of generous hugs and kisses.

Mema is passing on the blessing to the next generation. That's what Jacob did, too.

> Again today we have only one verse. Please read Hebrews 11:21. Write it below.

We pick back up with Jacob's story in Genesis 28:10. Jacob had fled to his mother's brother, Laban, to escape his brother who wanted to kill him. He was also looking for a wife from among his mother's people as his father had instructed him.

> Quickly read through Genesis 28:10-22. Now skim chapters 29-33. Write a summary of this section of Scripture here:

> In chapter 32, Jacob had an encounter with God. He realized that he and his entire family could have been killed, and he began to call on the God of his fathers. He began to acknowledge that all he had was from God. When Jacob wrestled with God, why do you think he sought God's blessing?

What did God change Jacob's name to?

Israel means "he struggles with God." In what way had Jacob struggled with God? Have you ever struggled with God?

Now read chapter 35. How many sons did Jacob have?

List the sons of Jacob below:

1.	7.
2.	8.
3.	9.
4.	10.
5.	11.
6.	12.

Now we are skipping over some of the stories of Israel's children in order to get to the passage referred to in Hebrews. Read Genesis chapter 48.

Reuben was the firstborn of Israel, but because of his sin, he lost the right of the firstborn. Joseph, through his sons Ephraim and Manasseh, received the double portion of inheritance and blessing from Israel instead. Ephraim and Manasseh were essentially chosen as Israel's own.

Why do you think Israel chose to make Joseph's sons like his own?

Now let's read the blessings bestowed on Israel's own sons in Genesis 49.

Notice that each son received the blessing that was appropriate to him. Those sons who were wicked (Reuben) or violent (Simeon and Levi) received blessings that sound more like curses, as their sins brought consequences. How thankful are you that although our sins may still bring consequences, through the blood of Jesus, we are blessed and not cursed!

Verse 26 tells us that Joseph received the greatest blessing because he was the son of Rachel, whom Jacob loved. (Benjamin was as well, but his birth led to her death.) Joseph received the promise of fruitfulness and strength and the help of the Almighty in his life.

But let's look at Judah. Read again the blessing of Judah in 49:8-12. The name Judah means "praise." Judah made some mistakes in his life, but verse 11 tells us "he will wash his garments in wine, his robes in the blood of grapes." This is a prophetic word that Judah would confess and repent and be washed in the blood of the Lamb. His line is the one through whom Jesus came.

> So how does all of this relate to the faith of Jacob as we read in Hebrews 11:21? Read Genesis 47:28-31. Why did Israel (Jacob) "worship as he leaned on the top of his staff"?

Israel worshiped the God who made the promise to his father, the God who had shown kindness and faithfulness to him, the God with whom he struggled and was blessed, and the God who promised that through his descendants all the earth would be blessed. He blessed his grandsons because he knew the promise was for them, too. Israel's faith was in the One whom he knew would keep His promises. And he believed that promise enough to pass it on to the next generation. What about you? With whom do you need to share God's promises today?

Weekend Devo *Faith and God's Word*

Well, here we are at the end of another week! It's time to sit back and reflect on what we have studied this week. Got your coffee? Good! Let's get started!

This week we have studied the faith of Sarah, who made some major mistakes in handling barrenness and her maidservant, Hagar. We have looked at the faith of Abraham and Sarah in their believing in a promise that they never saw come to pass. We studied the faith of Abraham who, when tested, was willing to sacrifice his son, because he believed so strongly in God's promise to him. We considered the faith of Isaac, who was deceived by his own wife and son. And we witnessed Jacob's blessing and passing on of the promise to his sons, even though some of them were major disappointments to him.

I think for us today, we need to reflect on our own lives. Surely each of us has faced struggling with our own sin, unfulfilled longing, testing, betrayal, or disappointment. You may be in one of these places now or perhaps more than one of them. If so, God's Word is such good news for us!

According to Hebrews, these people were considered persons of faith, not because their lives were perfect, but because they persevered in their belief. They clung to God's Word and His promise, even in the messiness of their lives. They valued the promises of God above what their eyes could see. That is the very definition of faith!

- We have many more promises of God written in His Word for us today. We can we rely on His Word above what we can see or feel!

Psalm 145:13b—"The Lord is faithful to all his promises and loving toward all he has made."

2 Corinthians 1:20—"For no matter how many promises God has made, they are 'yes' in Christ."

No matter what you are struggling with today, God has a promise in His Word for you. If you are struggling with sin and the pain of your mistakes, remember God is faithful to forgive those who come to Him in sincere repentance.

1 John 1:9—"If we confess our sins, he is faithful to forgive us our sins and purify us from all unrighteousness."

- If you are struggling with longings unfulfilled, remember that God is the source of all our hope.

Romans 5:5—"And hope does not disappoint us, because God has poured out his love into our hearts by the Holy Spirit, whom he has given us."

- If you are going through a time of testing, remember in whom we find our strength.

Isaiah 40:31—"But those who hope in the Lord will renew their strength. They will soar on wings like eagles; they will run and not grow weary, they will walk and not be faint."

- If you are facing deceit or betrayal by someone you love, remember that in Jesus we find peace to guard our hearts and minds.

Philippians 4:6-7—"Do not be anxious about anything, but in everything, by prayer and petition, with thanksgiving, present your requests to God. And the peace of God, which transcends all understanding, will guard your hearts and your minds in Christ Jesus."

- And if you are finding disappointment in the choices of your loved ones or feeling as if you have failed in your parenting, remember that God's grace will cover you.

Romans 5:20-21—"The law was added so that the trespass might increase. But where sin increased, grace increased all the more, so that just as sin reigned in death, so also grace might reign through righteousness to bring eternal life through Jesus Christ our Lord."

In our darkest moments, God's Word will bring us through. Hold fast to His promises, even in the face of contradictory evidence. Sarah was just a woman like you and me, and yet God called her faithful—not because she had it all together, but she trusted in a God who did.

> Application: Whatever doubt-filled moment you may find yourself in today, God has a promise for you in His Word. Whether you need forgiveness, hope, strength, peace, or grace, God has it! Use a concordance to look up Scriptures on whichever of those key words you need most right now. Copy those Scriptures onto index cards and post them where you will see them throughout the day—refrigerator, mirror, etc. You could frame one or more and put on your desk or bedside table. Keep God's promises before you. When doubts come, remember these people we have studied who surely had doubts, too. And then remember you serve the same God who called them faithful!

Small Group Ideas

- Use these questions for discussion.
  - Have you ever gotten tired of waiting on God and taken things into your own hands? How did that work out?
  - How can God use our mistakes for our good?
  - What are some longings that you have yet to see fulfilled?
  - Why is it so easy to focus on this life and forget about the one to come?
  - Have you ever faced a time that you knew God was testing your faith?
  - Has God ever made you retake a test that you failed?
  - How can you respond with faith in the face of betrayal?
  - How do you think God feels about you when you are in times of failure or discouragement?

- Print each of the following Scriptures on small pieces of paper or cardstock that can be drawn out of a basket. Have a time of worship at the close of your session and ask each participant to prayerfully come forward and draw out a Scripture. Ask God to give each woman the promise she needs for that moment. Pray for each other.
- Forgiveness: 1 John 1:9, 2 Corinthians 5:21, 1 John 1:7, 1 John 2:1, Psalms 130:4, Ephesians 1:7
- Hope: Romans 5:5, Psalm 62:5, Jeremiah 29:11, Psalm 25:3, Romans 15:13
- Strength: Isaiah 40:31, Psalm 46:1, Philippians 4:13, Psalm 73:26, Psalm 28:7
- Peace: Isaiah 26:3, Psalm 29:11, John 14:27, Philippians 4:6-7, John 16:33
- Grace: Romans 5:1-2, 2 Corinthians 9:8, 2 Corinthians 12:9, Ephesians 1:7, Hebrews 4:16, 2 Peter 3:18

Week 3

"For the Lord is good and his love endures forever; his faithfulness continues through all generations."

Psalm 100:5

Faith and God's Faithfulness

Day 1—A Sure Confidence

God is so faithful! He is so much better to us than we deserve, amen? Before we look at Joseph's life, I want us to take a look at each of our own. I am sure we can all think of times in which we may have felt like Joseph—hated by his brothers, accused of something he didn't do. Can you recall a time in your own life in which you were in a tough situation through no fault of your own?

If we're honest enough with ourselves, we can probably find that some fault lay with us in almost any situation. After all, even Joseph didn't have to brag about being his daddy's favorite. But there are some situations that are completely orchestrated by the enemy. In these times, we find it easier to question God.

Why did God let this happen? What am I supposed to do now? Does God even care?

Joseph had every right to feel that way, and perhaps we think we do, too. As we study Joseph's life, we will see that God didn't cause the evil done to him, but He surely used it for great good—in fact, He used it to bring life to his entire family. Maybe we can trust God to do the same for us.

Read Hebrews 11:22 and write it here.

Why was Joseph commended for his faith?

Let me summarize Joseph's story here. Joseph was favored by his father and hated by his brothers. They sold him into slavery, and he ended up in Egypt where he prospered because God was with him. He came to be in charge of the household of one of the pharaoh's officials, where he caught the eye of his wife. She accused him of inappropriate behavior and he was thrown in jail. But God was with him and showed him favor. Later he interpreted dreams by God's help and predicted a great famine. So Pharaoh put him in charge of the whole land. His brothers ended up in Egypt because of the famine, where Joseph finally revealed himself to them. In chapter 46, Israel and all of his family came to Egypt to live, and God confirmed His promise to Israel once again.

If you don't mind, I would like you to take a few minutes and skim over Genesis chapters 37 and 39-45. See if you can count the number of times Joseph was faced with a choice to do wrong or right. He faced mistreatment at the hands of his brothers, the merchants, Potiphar's wife, and the cupbearer. Write below how you think Joseph could have chosen to respond.

It's a long story, but it is a story of faith and trust in the God of his father. Joseph suffered greatly at the hands of his brothers and in prison because of Potiphar's wife, but God continued to show favor and blessing to him, just as He had promised. What seemed to be at risk, however, was the promised land of Canaan, for all of Abraham's descendants were now in Egypt.

Now let's read Genesis 50:15-26. Copy Genesis 50:20 here.

Why do you believe that Joseph was able to forgive his brothers for all that was done to him and still trust in God?

Have you ever had wrong done to you that changed the course of your life?

If you have, then know this: whether you have seen it happen yet or not, God is more than able to use the situation for your good. You may not see how, but just believe the truth of God's Word. His purposes in you will be fulfilled.

Read verse 24 again. Why do you think Joseph was able to "see" the exodus before it occurred?

Just as his father had done, he also gave instructions about his bones. Joseph knew that he would not live to see them return to Canaan, but he wanted his bones buried in the land of promise. This was an act of his faith. He believed that all of his family would one day return to that land because he believed the God who promised to be with him all his life. God had been faithful to Joseph in all that he had been through, even through all the wrong that was done to him. God used every evil act for good. Had Joseph not been sold into slavery by his brothers or thrown into prison by Potiphar, he would not have risen to the place of prominence that allowed him to save the entire nation of Israel during the famine.

God did not cause the evil that was done against Joseph, but He was able to turn it around and use it for good. And Joseph had faith that God would keep His promises—promises that began with Joseph's great-grandfather, Abraham. Because Joseph knew the God of the promise, he knew the promise would be fulfilled. Therefore, he could speak with confidence about the future of the nation of Israel.

Many hundreds of years later, Paul would write in Philippians 1:6 "being confident of this, that he who began a good work in you will carry it on to completion until the day of Christ Jesus."

Whatever work God has begun in you, you can be assured that he will be faithful to complete it, even if circumstances may appear contrary to the fact right now. You may not know how God will work it all out (Joseph knew nothing of Moses!) But like Joseph, you can speak with confidence of the future He has for you. If you know Jesus as your Lord and Savior, the promises of forgiveness, salvation, and eternal life are yours. God doesn't take back His promises. Even if you are still in Egypt right now. God finishes what He starts, and he will complete your story and bring you into the Promised Land.

Day 2—A Brave Choice

Has God ever called you out into the unknown? Several years ago our church took some of our youth on a retreat in the mountains. The leader of the retreat center took us on a hike one day. We walked and walked and finally came to the opening of a cave. He led us into the cave with the light from his flashlight. Once we got inside, he had us all sit down. Then he turned off the light. The darkness was overwhelming. I'm not particularly afraid of the dark, but this was a thick darkness. We could see absolutely nothing. My only consolation was that I could feel the people next to me and hear their voices.

The leader told us that he wanted us to go back out of the cave one by one, *on our own*, in the dark. We had to feel our way out. He was making a spiritual point about what it is like to be lost, but I will admit: I was terrified. I could handle it, no problem, if we all went out together. I wasn't afraid of the dark as much as the aloneness.

I don't remember who went first, but eventually it was my turn. As I stood, heart pounding, and started to find my way out, the leader began reciting Psalm 139. I read a Psalm every single day in my quiet time, and I have for years, so this Scripture was very familiar to me. Suddenly, I felt the peace that comes with having someone with you. I felt the Lord with me through His Word, a passage that I was very comfortable with. I was no longer afraid, and I confidently began to make my way back. As I walked further, his voice began to fade, but the cave then began to turn grey instead of black. I squinted and strained and realized that I could see light up ahead.

I was afraid, but God's Word gave me the courage to step out. What is the connection between faith and courage?

Our next verse in Hebrews is 11:23. Read the verse and answer the following questions:

What did Moses' parents do by faith?

48

They were able to do this for two reasons. What were they?
1.
2.

Let's read Exodus 1-2:10. Why did the king of Egypt want to kill the Hebrew baby boys (1:12)?

The Hebrews had been in Egypt for over 400 years. They left Canaan with about 70 men and they had grown to 600,000 men, not counting the women and children! (12:37.) The Egyptians had come to fear the Hebrews' numbers and power.

Why did the Hebrew women's midwives not obey the king's edict (1:17)?

What was the Pharaoh's new edict given in 1:22?

To whom was this new edict issued?

Exodus 2:2 says that when Moses' mother gave birth to him and saw that he was a "fine child," she hid him for three months. Hebrews says he was no ordinary child. Read Acts 7:20. What do you think it means that Moses was a fine child?

Apparently there was something about Moses that set him apart, even as a baby! Perhaps his parents could sense the anointing on him and knew that he was destined to be a great man used by God. Whatever the reason, they had faith that God would allow them to hide him for three months without his being discovered by the Egyptians, who would have killed him.

According to Hebrews 11:23, what other reason was given for the faith of Moses' parents?

They did not fear the king's edict! Why do you believe that this was so?

This generation of Hebrews had only heard about the promises of God to Abraham, Isaac, and Jacob. But remember that even though they had become slaves in Egypt, they had been fruitful and prospered. Like Joseph, the favor of God had been on them. The stories of the faith of their fathers had been passed down to them, so they knew that they would one day return to Canaan.

> What did Moses' mother do after three months when she knew she could hide him no longer?

What faith Moses' parents had that their child would be saved! God must have revealed to them that Moses would be the one whom God chose to lead His people out of Egypt and back into the Promised Land. I can't imagine what it would be like to place your three-month-old baby in a basket on the Nile and trust God to protect him, but that is exactly what they did.

The faith that God commends in Hebrews is a faith that trusts God with all the hopes and dreams of the future. This story is very reminiscent of Abraham trusting God with Isaac. How about you? Are there some dreams and hopes that you need to lay down and trust God with? I share this from my own heart. Some of us feel the need to be in control, even though we know that God is in control. I believe this need comes from fear that if we don't protect or hover over our promise, something might go wrong. But I am learning that God is faithful, and I can trust Him. He is completely trustworthy. You may need to say that out loud right now.

"God, you are completely trustworthy. I can trust you with my needs, my family, my finances, my health, my dreams."

Moses' parents trusted God with, not only their baby, but the hope of the nation. They were not afraid of the king's edict, because they knew the faithfulness of their God, even while they were still in captivity—slaves in a foreign land! They were able to step out in faith into the unknown to see God's plan fulfilled.

What are you afraid of? What has God called you to do that requires a brave choice? Remember the faithfulness of God in the past and the surety of His promise for the future. Then step out in faith. Just as surely as Baby Moses was safe in God's hands, so are you. Moses ended up exactly where he needed to be to fulfill God's plan for his life and for the nation.

Will you trust God to do the same in you?

Day 3—A Future Reward

I have a friend who once said that she couldn't understand why God wouldn't let her watch certain movies that she knew lots of other Christians watched. They were popular movies, but every time she started to watch one, she would feel convicted that God didn't want her to watch it.

God calls us believers to a higher standard than the world around us. Sometimes those in ministry are called to an even higher standard. Taking the high road isn't always easy, but there are blessings in store for those who sacrifice for His sake.

Do you sometimes feel that you have given up a lot to follow Christ? Forgiving others, turning the other cheek, loving our enemies, putting others ahead of ourselves, serving others, denying ourselves, walking away from gossip, refusing to cheat, lie, or steal from our employers—these are all actions God calls us to take as His followers.

So why do we? Because by faith we believe He has something far better in store for us.

> Let's begin by reading Hebrews 11:24-28. Why was Moses commended for his faith? Finish the following verses in your own words:
>
> 1. By faith Moses (verses 24-26)...
>
> 2. By faith he (verse 27)...
>
> 3. By faith he (verse 28)...

Let's look at each of these. First, Moses was commended for refusing to be identified as an Egyptian and choosing to be mistreated as a Hebrew slave. You probably already know Moses' story, but let's look briefly at selected passages in Exodus. Turn to Exodus and read 2:11-25.

Now read Acts 7:21-29. What we learn is that Moses could have stayed in Egypt and enjoyed the treasures and pleasures of being a member of royalty, but instead he came to the defense of one of his own people who was being mistreated. That landed him in a heap of trouble! He fled to Midian where some of the Hebrew descendants lived.

Next, Moses was commended for his faith in leaving Egypt. The Exodus passage says that Moses was afraid when he realized someone knew he had killed an Egyptian, but it doesn't say of whom he was afraid. Hebrews tells us he didn't fear the king's anger, so perhaps he feared the people. The Hebrews passage says he left Egypt out of perseverance because he saw "him who is invisible." Whom do you think Moses saw?

> Read Colossians 1:15 and write it here:

Moses saw Jesus and he knew God had called him to lead His people back to the Promised Land, and so he persevered. All the treasures of Egypt could not compare to the promise of God! Moses spent 40 more years in Midian, waiting for the time when God would use him to liberate His people.

The third reason Moses is commended for his faith is in keeping the Passover. Let's go back to Exodus and skim chapters 3-11. Summarize each chapter in just a few words. You can get the gist of the chapters from scanning the headings.

> Chapter 3 -
> Chapter 4 -
> Chapter 5 -
> Chapter 6 -
> Chapter 7 -
> Chapter 8 -
> Chapter 9 -
> Chapter 10-
> Chapter 11-

> Now read 12:1-13:16. God gave precise instructions to Moses for how to prepare the Passover so that the firstborn of all the Hebrews would be spared. Why do you believe this required great faith on Moses' part?

> Read the following Scriptures: Genesis 22:8, Isaiah 53:7, John 1:29, Acts 8:32, and 1 Corinthians 5:7.

The blood of the Passover Lamb saved them from death just as the blood of the Lamb saves us from death. Moses had the faith to believe that the Passover would save the Hebrew people and usher in their deliverance from Egypt into the Promised Land.

We can learn three important truths from the faith of Moses.

1. Faith sees that it is better to suffer disgrace and mistreatment from the world than to enjoy the treasures and pleasures of the world.

We must look ahead to our reward as Moses did. Moses was raised in the palace. He had the best education, the finest of everything. He gave up all of that when he defended the Israelite. He went from being a "prince" to being hunted by Pharaoh who tried to kill him. He went from the splendor of the palace to the desert of Midian, a dry and desolate place where he lived as an alien. He saw this trying time as of greater value than all the treasure of Egypt because he looked ahead to his reward. As Christians, we too have a great reward, but are we willing to suffer disgrace and mistreatment from the world, maybe even for years? Or do we desire the pleasures of the world instead? Only faith can look ahead to the reward and value it more.

2. Faith is able to persevere in doing what is right, even if we have to wait a long time to see God work.

Sometimes we have to do the right thing over and over and over again before we ever see the blessing from it. Sometimes God calls us to a higher standard than some of our friends, and we may not understand why. Our Christian friends may get away with things that God won't let us get away with. Sometimes we are mistreated by other Christians, but God makes us forgive them and keep doing the right thing and it is HARD! Real faith is able to keep doing the right thing, because our eyes are on our Savior and not ourselves.

3. Faith will follow the Word of God and trust the result to Him.

God gave Moses very precise instructions for the Passover, and Moses followed them completely. He knew it was a matter of life and death to everyone around him. Moses knew the Lord well enough to trust His Word. He believed by faith that if he kept the Passover as God instructed, not only would the Hebrews be spared, but Pharaoh would finally let the people go. His obedience was a matter of salvation and deliverance.

Did you know that our obedience to the Word of God could be a matter of life and death, salvation and deliverance, to the lives of those around us? The results are not up to us. Some people will respond and some won't. But God calls us to live our lives as a testimony to those around us and to love them with His love. That's the only way salvation and deliverance will come! God's Word is holy and right and true. We need to read it, breathe it, live it, love it, obey it, and share it with a lost and dying world. The blood of the Lamb is still able to save and heal and deliver!

Lord, may our obedience to Your Word be a witness that will set the captive free!

Day 4—Two "Impossible" Obstacles

Have you ever faced an impossible obstacle? My father was a Vietnam veteran with PTSD. He suffered with depression and alcoholism in his latter years. Once when he was going through a particularly rough time, he made some suicidal threats which frightened us, so we removed his guns from the house. My sister and I wanted him to get treatment at the VA, but without his voluntary admission, he would have to be involuntarily committed. It was one of the most difficult times of our lives.

We live in a small town, so we were able to talk to the sheriff and he agreed to help us. We found out that Daddy still had a shotgun that we didn't know about. Bringing in an armed, depressed, drunk, military veteran against his will would be almost impossible. If they drove up in his yard, the situation could lead to suicide by cop, so the sheriff's department came up with a plan.

They decided to send one of their deputies who had just returned from Iraq, wearing his fatigues and on foot. He would knock on Daddy's door after dark and explain that he was just returning from Iraq, had run out of gas, and needed Daddy's help—something Daddy would not have refused. Still, there was no guarantee this plan would work. Daddy was not in his right mind at the time. I had visions of shots being fired and my Daddy dying that night.

While all of this action was going down, I was on my knees beside my bed, praying and quoting Scriptures over my father. Finally we got a phone call. When the deputy walked up to the house, Daddy was not home. The deputy waited quietly in the neighbor's yard behind the bushes until Daddy drove up. He was then able to walk up to him and secure him without a fight. Daddy's life was spared, and he went to the hospital that night to get help.

As the Israelites followed God out of Egypt, they faced some "impossible" obstacles, too.

Today we will study two verses, both of them dealing with an impossible barrier—a sea and a wall. Read Hebrews 11:29-30.

> First, let's look at the Hebrews facing the Red Sea. We pick up where we left off yesterday at Exodus 13:17. Begin there and read through Exodus 14:31.

Why did God lead them through the Red Sea instead of by a shorter route (13:17)?

How did God protect and provide for the Israelites as they left Egypt (13:21-22)?

Why did God harden the Egyptians' hearts and cause them to pursue the Israelites (14:4, 17-18)?

How did the Israelites respond when they realized they were being pursued (14:10-12)?

Sometimes God takes us through a journey that is difficult for us when it seems there could have been a much easier way! We oftentimes respond like the Israelites—afraid, even though we know that God has been providing for us and protecting us all along. Like Moses, God is saying to us, "Do not be afraid. Stand firm and see the deliverance the Lord will bring you."

I find it interesting that even after their complaints and fears, God provided the pillar of cloud to protect them from the Egyptians. Then he completely delivered them and received all the glory. God didn't give up on them. He still came through for them and led them through an impossible situation! Seas don't part in the natural! It was a supernatural, divine intervention of God. And God's faithless people were commended for their faith in Hebrews! Why? Because they did it afraid. They may have had moments of doubt, but when it came time, they moved ahead in obedience! And God moved in and set them free.

From there the Israelites journeyed to Mt. Sinai where God gave them the Ten Commandments and instructions for the Tabernacle and worship. God provided food, water, clothing, and shelter. They never lacked, and yet they struggled with unbelief and doubted God's faithfulness. Even in their murmuring and complaining, God continued to provide for them as He promised, but He didn't allow them to go up and possess the land. Israel ended up taking forty years to make an eleven day journey to Canaan. They wandered in the wilderness, because although God wanted them to enter His rest, His rest would only come through trust. When that generation died out, God raised up two men with faith to lead them into the Promised Land: Joshua and Caleb. Moses' place of leadership was taken over by Joshua.

Turn to Joshua 5:13. Jericho was the closest Canaanite stronghold and the first place scouted by Joshua. We will come back to that tomorrow, but let's begin today and read 5:13-6:27. Whose direction was Joshua following (see verse 14)?

Describe Joshua's strange military strategy given to him by the Lord.

Can you imagine the response Joshua got from the men when he told them the strategy for conquering Jericho? It must have seemed foolish to march around a city and blow horns and shout. But sometimes God calls us to do things that may seem foolish to us but have spiritual significance to Him. Read 1 Corinthians 1:25. The key to the walls coming down was the faith and obedience of His people.

There is an important lesson here. At the first wall (the Red Sea) God brought them through, despite their murmuring in order to show His glory to the Egyptians and His power and faithfulness to His people. Then after the Israelites continued in unbelief, they were not allowed to enter the Promised Land. Only when a new generation of men of faith came along did God lead them in, and then only through a means that required a display of their faith—a strategy that in the natural would have seemed foolish, but through eyes of faith, simply required trust.

What can we learn about faith? It is by faith that the Israelites crossed the Red Sea on dry ground—the faith of Moses and the faith of the people to follow even though they were afraid.

It is by faith that the walls of Jericho came down—the faith of Joshua and the faith of the men who followed him and obeyed the instructions of the Lord. The common factor was obedience as a result of faith. When the Israelites failed to obey, they failed to succeed.

What kind of "impossible obstacle" are you facing? It may seem like a barrier as big as the Red Sea or the walls of Jericho that you see no way to overcome. Luke 1:37 reads "For nothing is impossible for God." In Luke 18:27 Jesus said, "What is impossible for men is possible for God." We may have a small faith but if we place it in a BIG God whom we know is more than able, we will see the deliverance of the Lord. But it *will* require obedience on our part.

When faced with a "Red Sea" or a "wall of Jericho," we must humble ourselves, seek the Lord, and pray to God, knowing that we can't, but He can. What is impossible with man is possible with God. Give it to the Lord in prayer, and then wait on an answer. And no matter how silly or foolish that answer may sound, follow God completely! He will lead you through and bring you out on the other side. And when He does, give Him all the glory!

Day 5—A Faith That Saves

The story of Rahab is one of an unbeliever coming to know the one true God, solely on the basis of the news that traveled to her. I love that! Have you ever been deeply affected by someone else's testimony? Spend a few minutes reflecting on that person's faith story. Why did it impact you the way it did?

Let's read Hebrews 11:31. Why is Rahab commended for her faith?

Turn to Joshua 2:1-24 and let's read her story. Rahab was a prostitute, but according to historians like Josephus, she was also an innkeeper. This explains why the spies were staying with her. The spies were looking for information about the city and its inhabitants. Or perhaps they went there knowing she was a prostitute and hoping to overhear conversations of the enemy there. Either way, God led the spies to her house.

Somehow the king of Jericho found out about the spies and demanded that she send them out, but Rahab covered for them and hid them.

Copy below Rahab's confession to the spies in verses 9-11.

I know that…

We have heard…

Rahab not only admitted that she knew about the God of the Israelites, but in verse 11, she confessed that He is the one true God, and she lived among a polytheistic people (those who worship many gods)!

Why was Rahab willing to risk her life for these men that she did not even know?

She revealed the key information that the Israelites needed for conquest: the Canaanites were afraid of the Israelites. In exchange, the spies agreed to save her and her family when the conquest took place (Joshua 6:17-25).

Read James 2:25. James doesn't condone her occupation. She was a new believer! But her strong faith in God was extraordinary for a woman of her background and nationality, and therefore God considered her righteous.

Where else do we see Rahab in the Bible? Matthew 1:5—the genealogy of Jesus! Only God could take a pagan prostitute and make her a woman of God! Why? Because she believed!

Rahab became a believer in the one true God because of the testimony of the Israelites and their relationship with God. Word had spread among those in Jericho of how God had brought the Israelites up out of Egypt and through the Red Sea on dry ground; how God had spared them from the hand of pharaoh; and how God had led them to success in battle against foreign kings. She had only heard about their God and His faithfulness, and she believed!

Are we spreading the good news of what Christ has done in our lives? Are we a living testimony of His kindness and faithfulness so that others will hear and believe?

Or do we just complain when things don't go our way and gossip about others when we are around unbelievers? If that is the case, we are not showing them the truth about our God. We need to be very intentional about the news that travels from us and from our churches so that others, like Rahab, are hearing the truth about the one true God.

We are surrounded by Rahabs every day—men and women who live in a culture in which many gods are worshiped. Like Rahab, they may only need to hear of the supernatural goodness of our God, to have faith in Him. Are we living our lives in such a way that others know we serve a God who saves?

He has released us from slavery to sin, parted some Red Seas in our lives, and led us to victory in battle against the enemy. So word should be traveling about our God like it did then.

"How beautiful on the mountains are the feet of those who bring good news" (Isaiah 52:7). Let's start bringing our world some good news!

Weekend Devo *Faith and God's Faithfulness*

Here we are at the end of another week! Time to sit back and reflect over what we have learned about faith and the faithfulness of our God!

On day 1, we learned about Joseph and his choice to persevere in doing what is right even in the face of great trials. Next, we studied the response of Moses' parents in choosing faith over fear. On day 3, we looked at Moses himself and the choices he made to choose suffering over sin. After that, we studied the Hebrews when they chose to believe God to do the impossible. Last, we looked at Rahab, a woman who chose to believe the truth about the one true God.

Did you notice what each of these narratives had in common? Choices! But not just arbitrary choices without a basis in truth—no, these were choices made based on the faithfulness of God.

We are faced with hundreds of choices every day—some important, some not so important. What do we base our choices on? God gave us free will. We are allowed to make our own choices, but that means that we can choose to follow our own hearts, our own desires, and our own way.

These men and women made choices that God commended in Hebrews 11, so I think it is worth our time to consider how we might also make choices that God will bless. How do we do that? By basing our choices on God's faithfulness, too!

1. ***God is faithful to work all things together for our good, and He will finish what He starts in us.***
   "But Joseph said to them, 'Don't be afraid. Am I in the place of God? You intended to harm me, but God intended it for good to accomplish what is now being done, the saving of many lives'" (Genesis 50:19-20).

   "And we know that in all things God works for the good of those who love him, who have been called according to his purpose" (Romans 8:28).

   "Being confident of this, that he who began a good work in you will carry it on to completion until the day of Christ Jesus" (Philippians 1:6).

2. ***God is faithful to do in us what we cannot do on our own.***
   "So do not fear, for I am with you; do not be dismayed, for I am your God. I will strengthen you and help you; I will uphold you with my righteous right hand" (Isaiah 41:10).

   "He gives strength to the weary and increases the power of the weak. Even youths grow tired and weary, and young men stumble and fall; but those who hope in the Lord will renew their strength. They will soar on wings like eagles; they will run and not grow weary, they will walk and not be faint" (Isaiah 40:29-31).

"I can do everything through him who gives me strength" (Philippians 4:13).

3. ***God is faithful to bless us when we choose to suffer rather than enjoy worldly pleasures.***
"But rejoice that you participate in the sufferings of Christ, so that you may be overjoyed when his glory is revealed. If you are insulted because of the name of Christ, you are blessed, for the Spirit of glory and of God rests on you" (1 Peter 1:13-14).

"I consider that our present sufferings are not worth comparing to the glory that will be revealed in us" (Romans 8:18).

4. ***God is faithful to lead us through what He calls us to. We see the obstacle; God sees the possible.***
"For nothing is impossible for God" (Luke 1:37).

"Jesus said, 'What is impossible with men is possible with God'" (Luke 18:27).

5. ***God is faithful to rescue those who put their trust in Him.***
"The righteous man is rescued from trouble..." (Proverbs 11:8a).

"For he has rescued us from the dominion of darkness and brought us into the kingdom of the Son he loves, in whom we have redemption, the forgiveness of sins" (Colossians 1:13-14).

I'm so glad that God calls us to faith in the unseen, but not the unknown! Our faith is not blind! It is based on the truth of who God is, and it is confirmed to us through His Word. Yes, God is calling you and me to make right choices, but these choices are based on His faithfulness, not our meager faith.

Application: What choices are you facing right now? What do you need to believe God for? Will you choose to base your decisions on the faithfulness of God and His truth? Take a moment and write out what that would look like in your life.

Small Group Ideas

- Use these questions for discussion:
  - Have you ever faced a situation in which you had to choose to persevere in doing right, even when you were being treated wrongly?
  - How did you feel? What role did prayer and Scripture play in helping you make the right decisions?
  - Have you ever allowed fear to prevent you from doing something you thought God was calling you to do?

- Why is it difficult to choose suffering over an easier way out? In what ways do others, the devil, or our own thoughts make the choice more difficult?
- What are some of the benefits that come from choosing God's ways?
- Have you ever seen God come through in a miraculous way? What role did your faith play in that miracle?

- This week's small group session is a great opportunity to minister to one another. Break into pairs or triplets and share with your group at least one decision you are struggling with. Encourage one another to choose God's ways. Pray for each person in the group to have the strength to do what God is calling her to do. Close by singing "Great Is Thy Faithfulness" together.

Week 4

"Therefore, since through God's mercy we have
this ministry, we do not lose heart."

2 Corinthians 4:1

Faith and Ministry

Day 1—A New Name

Were you ever called names as a child? Did you let those names determine how you thought about yourself? Perhaps you were characterized as overweight, skinny, dumb, or fearful. Sticks and stones and all that, but we know it's not true. Words do hurt. Probably the most hurtful names are the ones we give ourselves.

The great news is that God is in the business of changing names—from Jacob to Saul, God gives names that reflect who He has called us to be. Our self-worth cannot be based on anything other than what God says about us. Like Gideon in our lesson today, God sees our potential and calls us out to follow Him in faith. We will only be successful in ministry when we believe God's voice and not another's.

These next verses will give us several days of study! Let's read Hebrews 11:32-33. "And what more shall I say? I do not have time to tell about Gideon, Barak, Samson, Jephthah, David, Samuel and the prophets, who through faith conquered kingdoms, administered justice, and gained what was promised; who shut the mouths of lions."

Gideon's story is in Judges chapters 6 and 7.

During this period of Israelite history, the Israelites repeatedly went through a cycle of sin, punishment, and deliverance as God would raise up someone to lead or "judge" the people. This is where the title "Judges" comes from. When Gideon's story begins, we find the Israelites in a period of sin and punishment at the hands of the Midianites. The Midianites were so oppressive that the Israelites were hiding in caves! They were so desperate that they had begun to cry out to God for help.

When God spoke to Gideon, he was threshing wheat in a winepress! Threshing wheat was usually done out in the open so that the wind could blow the chaff from the grain when it was winnowed or tossed in the air. Out of fear of being exposed to the Midianites, Gideon was hiding in a winepress where grapes would normally be stomped, trying to thresh wheat.

What did the angel of the Lord call him in 6:12?

Gideon was a mighty warrior in God's eyes, even though he was fearful of the enemy. God called him what he knew he could be with God's help. What did the angel of the Lord call Gideon to do?

What was Gideon's response?

Gideon was so afraid that he asked for a sign, which the Lord gave him. He began to grow in courage after the sign, so he tore down the idols, but he did it at night, because he was still somewhat afraid.

What important event happened to Gideon in 6:34?

Even with the courage of the Spirit of the Lord, Gideon still asked God for a sign before he would go to battle against the enemy. Once God gave him the sign, Gideon became a mighty warrior, indeed!

Why did the Lord make Gideon pare his army down to only 300 men?

How did the Lord encourage Gideon to go forward even in his fear (7:10-11)?

How did Gideon respond to this encouragement in verse 15?

What was Gideon's military strategy?

Why do you think Gideon was successful?

Compare Gideon's words in 6:15 with his words in 7:15. God took a man hiding out, trying to thresh wheat in a winepress, called him a "mighty warrior," and then turned him into a fearless leader who rescued his people from the hands of the enemy. What made the difference?

I believe we can learn three important truths from this lesson.

1. The words God speaks over us are the only ones that matter. God called Gideon "mighty warrior." He calls us "child of God," "beloved," "Bride of Christ," "friend," and so many others. We have to tune out the names the enemy gives us and listen to the "voice of truth."
2. It was the Spirit of the Lord on Gideon that finally empowered him to go forward with courage and lead his people. As believers, we have the Spirit of God inside us to empower us to follow him in ministry.
3. Hebrews calls Gideon a man of faith, even though he had doubts and fears. God understood, and God helped him overcome those doubts and fears and used him in spite of them. By faith, we need to live by the Word of God empowered by the Spirit of God. Then God can use us to overcome the enemy, and He will bring victory to our lives!

Day 2—A Willing Follower

Many years ago, as I was first starting out in ministry as a worship leader and music director in my church, I made some decisions that proved to be disastrous. I did not have a clear understanding of ministry and leadership. I incorrectly assumed that since I had been asked to serve in this position, and I knew what the ministry requirements were, then I could just plan anything I wanted without involving the pastor in my decisions. I honestly thought that I was fulfilling my duties in that way.

I proceeded to plan an entire program that would include music and Scriptural readings as an evangelistic outreach to our community. I worked with our praise team and readers, made flyers, organized a group to go door-to-door and give out the flyers, and then had the service announced in the bulletin. Which was the first time the pastor heard or saw anything about it.

It was a great idea, but God didn't bless it because I didn't go through the proper channels. God has an order and purpose to everything He does. Today's lesson may seem unusual because a man is following a woman. But as we read, we will see that God had a purpose in it.

The next man in this Scripture is Barak. We find his story in Judges 4.

> Where was Israel in the cycle of sin, punishment, and deliverance at the beginning of this story?

> Why were the Israelites so afraid of Jabin and his army?

> How long had the Israelites been oppressed by them?

> Who was Deborah?

What is a prophetess?

Why do you think Barak, a military leader, refused to go into battle without Deborah?

Deborah rebuked Barak for his lack of faith (perhaps in himself), but she sent him out, reminding him in verse 14 that the Lord had gone ahead of him. When Barak went into battle, the enemy had been warned by Heber the Kenite. Barak had 10,000 men, but Sisera, captain of Jabin's army, had 900 iron chariots! God routed the enemy and brought a storm that flooded the Kishon River, causing the chariots to get stuck (see chapter 5 where the whole story is recounted again in a poem). Jabin's army fell to the sword, but Sisera fled on foot.

What happened to Sisera?

Why do you think Barak is included in the Hebrews "Hall of Faith"?

He apparently is commended for his faith in "conquering kingdoms, administering justice, and gaining what was promised." And yet because he wouldn't go into battle without Deborah, he lost the honor of being the one to kill the captain of the enemy's army—to a woman!

I believe he is commended for his faith because he trusted in God's power to bring victory. Maybe he wanted Deborah there because she was the one speaking for God, and he didn't trust his own judgment in battle. He put his faith into action by being willing to follow the leader, even if she was a woman. The leader of Israel was Deborah, the judge and prophetess for the nation, but the one commended for his faith in Hebrews is Barak. So what does God want us to learn about faith? Faith is shown not by whether or not we doubt, but whether or not we obey!

Do you trust in God's power to bring victory in your own life? If Barak had not had faith in God, he would not have led 10,000 men down a mountain towards a 20-year enemy with 900 "tanks"! Sometimes it may seem that we face a huge enemy, but we have to remember that the victory lies with our Lord. Like Barak, we need the prophetic voice of the Lord (God's Word) to go with us as well.

In chapter 5, both Deborah and Barak sing praises to God for all that he has done. God will use those whom He knows will give Him the praise!

If you are facing a battle with the enemy, remember that you are not alone. God and His mighty Word are with you to face the enemy, just as Deborah the prophetess of God was with Barak. We need only to follow our Leader, trust in His Word, believe in His power to overcome, and give Him the praise when He does. That is faith in action!

Day 3—A Mighty Strength

What does it mean to be set apart for God?

Samson's birth was announced to his barren mother by an angel, much like John the Baptist's birth was announced to Elizabeth. Samson's mother was instructed to bring him up in the Nazirite vow, just as Elizabeth was instructed about her son (Luke 1:11-17). Samson was chosen to deliver the Israelites from the Philistines; John was chosen to announce the coming of the One who would deliver the Israelites from sin.

Being set apart for God through this vow simply meant that God had a special purpose for these men that required their separateness from the world. God has used many great men and women, but not all of them were set apart with this vow. So why do you think God chose these men? God is omniscient, or all-knowing. Perhaps he knew that had they not been set apart from birth, they would have strayed from His calling. For Samson, however, following this vow meant life or death. For only in obedience to the vow would Samson be empowered to what God called him to do.

We begin today with Samson's story found in Judges 13-16. The Lord appeared to Manoah and his wife and told them that though she was barren, she would give birth to a son. They were to bring him up as a Nazirite. *Nazirite* comes from the Hebrew word for "separated." It was a voluntary vow one would make to God for a specific period of time. The vow included not drinking wine, not cutting one's hair, and abstaining from anything unclean. Samson's vow, however, was not commanded by God and was to last his lifetime.[10]

> Where was Israel in the cycle of sin, punishment, and deliverance?

> Who was oppressing the Israelites and for how long?

God raised up Samson and consecrated him to be the Judge who would deliver Israel from the hands of the Philistines. Read 13:25, 14:6, and 14:19. What happened in each of these verses?

The Spirit of the Lord gave Samson great strength, but God's purpose in that strength was to subdue the Philistines.

What was Samson's great weakness?

How did God intend to use that weakness?

Samson was just looking for revenge on the Philistines, but God's purpose was to use him to conquer them. Because of his weakness for women, Samson gave up the secret of his strength, which was his hair that had never been cut as part of his Nazirite vow. Delilah got the secret out of him, and he was then subdued by the Philistines.

The Philistines seemed to have won the battle with the Israelites. Their great, powerful leader had been captured and his eyes gouged out. But meanwhile his hair had grown back, bringing back the mighty strength of God.

How did God use Samson to bring judgment on the Philistines?

How many men and women were there when Samson crashed the temple?

How many years had Samson led the Israelites?

This is such an interesting account of the time of the Judges, because Samson was set apart for the Lord, yet he made so many selfish decisions, led by his flesh more than by the Spirit. Yet when he was led by the Spirit, God gave him great power to defeat his enemies.

He is commended in Hebrews for his faith, so we must see where in his life Samson showed such faith. We don't see much about his relationship with the Lord, except that the Spirit often came on him with great power. Then on his last day, he prayed and asked God to strengthen him one more time so he could get one last act of revenge on the Philistines, who were not just his enemies, but the enemies of God. God granted him that power and 3,000 were killed.

So Samson's faith lay in his trust that God would empower him with his Spirit and give him strength to accomplish His purposes. Samson's motives may seem selfish to us, but had they not accomplished God's purposes, God probably would not have granted his requests, both for the Philistine wife and for strength in the end.

Faith comes from God. It is a special gift of God that comes to those who believe He will do what He says. Samson believed God would come through for him in the end. As the writer of Hebrews says, "through faith [he] conquered kingdoms, administered justice, and gained what was promised." The Israelites cried out to be delivered from the oppression of their enemy. God heard their cry and sent Samson. In his lifetime, he killed over 4,000 Philistines with his own hands. The Spirit of God was on Samson for a purpose, and by faith Samson fulfilled that purpose.

God calls us to be set apart for His kingdom purposes. Read 2 Corinthians 6:14-18.

Only when we separate ourselves unto the Lord will we be empowered to fulfill the call of God on our lives. Ministry is about walking with God and carrying out His mission in this world. Do you want to be on mission with God? Separate yourself from anything that keeps you from total obedience to Him.

Day 4—A Rash Promise

Do you have a past of which you are ashamed? Some of the greatest men and women of God came from shameful pasts. They could have let the pain of their past define them, but instead they allowed God to use their pain or their shame to minister to others. Sometimes our past hurts and mistakes are the very experiences God uses to give us passion. We can identify with someone else's story. We can point to ourselves as examples of God's grace. We can understand someone else's pain.

Our next man of faith is Jephthah. For his story, let's read Judges 11:1-12:7.

Where was Israel in the cycle of sin, punishment, and deliverance?

Who wanted to make war with them?

Jephthah was despised and driven away by his brothers because he was the son of a prostitute and not their mother. Talk about a shameful past! His mother was a whore. His own brothers didn't acknowledge him, and apparently his own father didn't either. He was a social outcast and ineligible for his father's inheritance. But where he settled, men followed him. He was a natural leader! God called him a mighty warrior. When his people were threatened by the Ammonites, they didn't have the courage to face them, so they called on Jephthah.

How did Jephthah respond to them?

They promised to make Jephthah their leader, so he reluctantly agreed. What was his strategy with the king of Ammon?

Jephthah defended the right of the Israelites to possess the land God gave them. He tried to reason with them, but they ignored him. What happened to Jephthah in 11:29?

What vow did Jephthah make to the Lord?

This was a common practice among the Israelites and showed his dedication to the Lord. He probably expected an animal to come out of the house, as would have been common in his day, but what happened instead?

Jephthah did defeat the Ammonites through the power of God, but he returned to find his daughter coming out to meet him. Jephthah was true to his vow to God. The Bible does not say that he literally sacrificed her. Some scholars believe that he forced her to consecrate herself as a virgin and never marry to carry on his family line. This seems to fit her lamenting with her girlfriends that she would never marry, but not that she would die. The Bible never advocates human sacrifice.

After this battle, Jephthah faced another threat from the men of Ephraim, who got mad because he didn't invite them to the battle. Again he tried to reason with them, but then he led his men against them and killed them.

So what can we learn from the faith of Jephthah? Name some strengths of Jephthah:

What were his weaknesses?

How long did Jephthah rule over Israel?

Jephthah was a mighty warrior, a natural leader whom men followed, and a diplomat who tried to reason with the enemy before engaging in battle. He defended the Lord and their land against the Ammonites and clearly acknowledged the hand of God in giving the land to the Israelites. He called on the Lord and trusted God to be with him in battle, knowing that he could not defeat the enemy in his own strength.

This is the faith Jephthah was commended for—conquering kingdoms, administering justice, and gaining what was promised.

What can we learn from Jephthah?

1. He may have been rejected by his family, but God had a plan for his life. We, too, may face rejection or pain from our past, but we can overcome and be used by God to accomplish His purposes. The very pain or shame we have suffered, God can use to minister to someone else. Each of us is broken is some way. Rather than letting out past define us, we can let it refine us and make us into instruments of blessing to others and praise to God for what He has brought us through.

2. In the face of opposition, we can boldly take a stand for God and his Word and trust that God will see us through. He will empower us to stand against the enemy. He is our Defender.

3. We should not let our zeal or pride cause us to make rash promises to God. We should just follow God and trust Him with the results. He will empower us to serve Him without our having to make promises we may not be able or willing to keep.

   1 Samuel 15:22 says, "Does the Lord delight in burnt offerings and sacrifices as much as in obeying the Lord? To obey is better than sacrifice, and to heed is better than the fat of rams." We need to walk by faith in obedience and trust God with the rest.

Day 5—A Heart for God

Our next man of faith is David, and besides Jesus, he is my favorite person in the Bible. We would have to read all of 1 and 2 Samuel, 1 Chronicles, and most of the Psalms to get a full picture of David's life! Few men have done so much, so well. David was a shepherd, poet, musician, soldier, prophet, priest, king, administrator, hero, and friend. Rather than read all of these passages, we will summarize David's life and then read a few select passages.

David was the son of Jesse of Bethlehem and was anointed by the prophet Samuel to succeed Saul as king. After the period of the Judges, the Israelites began to cry out for a king as the other nations had. God warned them of the dangers of having a man as king rather than having a theocracy, where God is their King and uses men and women to lead them, but he finally gave them over to their desires. Saul was anointed as the first king, but failed to follow God completely. God chose David to be the next king but only after the death of Saul. Saul was jealous of David because of his success and fame in killing Goliath and tried to have David killed, but David refused to retaliate and waited on God's timing. He was a great friend to Saul's son Jonathan, who was very loyal to David as well.

Saul died and David succeeded him as king. He defeated the Philistines and won back Israel's land, set up a capital at Jerusalem, "the city of David," and enlarged the borders of the nation by defeating many enemies. He had the Ark of the Covenant brought back to Israel at Jerusalem and made plans to have a temple constructed for God. God told David that his son Solomon would be the one to build the temple, but he promised David that his throne and kingdom would be established forever, a promise that God kept through His Son Jesus, a descendant of David.

David was a great man of God, but he was not without sin. He slept with a married woman and she became pregnant. Knowing they both faced the death penalty under law, David had her husband killed in battle by putting him on the front line. He essentially broke the sixth, seventh, ninth, and tenth commandments. In 2 Samuel 12, David was confronted by the prophet Nathan. Read 2 Samuel 12:1-13. Now read Psalm 51, which was written following this confrontation with Nathan.

What was David's response to Nathan and to God?

Read 1 Samuel 13:13-14. These are the words of the prophet Samuel to Saul when he was king. Now read Acts 13:22. God says that David was a man

_____.

David suffered greatly after this sin. The child of Bathsheba died. His son Amnon raped his daughter Tamar; then his son Absalom killed his son Amnon. Absalom revolted and tried to usurp the throne from his father David. Two more uprisings followed. Finally, David had his son Solomon anointed to be the next king before his death.

There are many examples of David's faith—fighting Goliath, trusting God when Saul was trying to kill him, going into battle against the enemies of Israel—but the greatest act of faith was his humble submission and repentance. David trusted that God would forgive him and heal him. In the Psalms he poured his heart out to God, and even in times of depression, sickness, and oppression from enemies, his faith in God was always strong.

Read Psalm 3 which David wrote when Absalom rose up against him. How did David show his faith in God?

Read Psalm 27. David was a man like any other man and he sinned like any other sinner. The difference in David is that his faith was in the Lord. No matter what happened in his life, he loved God. Write Psalm 27:4 below:

We all sin. We intend to do right and end up doing wrong. We fail, we get it wrong, we say the wrong things, we make bad decisions, and God knows it. In the midst of failure, God is just looking for an honest heart—one that will agree with Him about our sin and turn from it.

David was a man after God's very own heart. I pray that each of us will walk in righteousness and not repeat David's mistakes. But if you, like me, look back and know that you already have, then I pray God will give you a heart that seeks Him.

We are all sinners. But may we all have a heart to say, like David, if I can only have one thing, let it be to dwell in the presence of my God.

Weekend Devo *Faith and Ministry*

Well, here we are at the end of yet another week of Bible study. Let me congratulate you for staying committed thus far! God will bless your efforts to study His Word and know Him more.

As we look at the relationship between faith and ministry, let's review what we learned this week from our men of faith. From Gideon we learned that we must find our identity in who God says we are. From Barak, we learned that we must be willing to follow those whom God gives to lead us. Through Samson we learned that we must be set apart by God for His purposes. In Jephthah we learned that we can serve God regardless of our past. And in David we learned about having a heart for God and a willingness to repent.

Now let's apply this to our lives.

What is ministry? We are all called to some type of ministry. The word *ministry* comes from the Greek word *diakonia* which means "to serve."[11] We are all called by God to serve Him in His Kingdom. When we surrender our lives to Jesus Christ, we are choosing to be His follower or His servant and to do His will. That means that, like the twelve apostles, we will follow Jesus wherever He leads us.

Take a look at this passage in Luke 17:7-10:

"'Suppose one of you had a servant plowing or looking after the sheep. Would he say to the servant when he comes in from the field, "Come along now and sit down to eat"? Would he not rather say, "Prepare my supper, get yourself ready and wait on me while I eat and drink; after that you may eat and drink"? Would he thank the servant because he did what he was told to do? So you also, when you have done everything you were told to do, should say, "We are unworthy servants; we have only done our duty."'"

That's Jesus talking to us. So what has He told us to do? Well, in the Great Commission in Matthew 28:18-20, Jesus tells us to go and make other disciples and tell them what we have learned about following Jesus. The word *disciple* simply means a fully-devoted follower. So basically, once we become a follower of Jesus we should be busy doing our Father's business—making other disciples. That will look different for different people based on the gifts and abilities He has given each of us, but the goal should be the same.

So many times we spin our wheels trying to figure out what our "gift" is instead of just following Jesus day by day. I know for me, I waste too much time worrying over my own fears and insecurities instead of focusing on the needs around me. Oftentimes, the ministry is right in front of us, but we are too busy focusing on our needs to notice.

For today, let's just look at a few points from this week's study.

1. **Our sense of self-worth must come from who God says we are and not how the enemy or the world defines us.** This thought process will only come from time spent in God's Word. Just as Gideon needed to hear God's voice encouraging him and calling him a mighty man of valor, so we will need to listen to God's voice daily through His Word. God defines our worth through the price He paid for us.

2. **We must be willing to follow.** We must be born-again believers in and followers of the Lord Jesus Christ. And we must be willing to follow the authorities that God places in our lives. We can't learn to lead until we can submit and follow. Deborah was a woman, but she was God's chosen instrument to serve as a judge of Israel. Barak may have seemed like a coward, but he was putting his faith into action. So we, too, must be humble enough to follow those whom God sends to lead.

3. **We must be set apart for God's purposes.** We can't ride the fence with one foot in the Church and one foot in the world. James says a double-minded man is unstable in all that he does (1:8). If we want to follow Jesus, we must be all-in, 100%, set apart for God to use us as He sees fit. If we are to make disciples, then the world must see something different in us, just as Samson was set apart through the Nazarite vow. Our set-apartness comes through surrender to the Holy Spirit and His work in our lives.

4. **We can't allow our past to define our future.** Jephthah didn't have a great start in life, but he was determined to be on the Lord's side. The enemy (Satan) will use our upbringing, dysfunctional families, and past sins to convince us that we are of no use to God. That is a lie from the pit of hell. God has a plan and purpose for each of us, and if he calls you to do it, He will see you through it.

5. **We must have a heart for God and a willingness to repent.** Guess what? You are still a sinner. I am still a sinner. But if I have a heart for God and a willingness to repent, God can use me to do anything! Keep short accounts with God. As soon as you are aware of sin, confess it and turn away from it. Without a heart that is sensitive to and cooperative with the Holy Spirit, we will do very little for the Lord.

I believe that you want to serve God well. You want to do your duty and make Him proud, right? Know this: He loves you no matter what! God's love is unconditional. He can take your past and make it your passion. Don't let fear, insecurity, pride, the world, the devil, or your sin keep you from ministry.

> Application: Look around you today and be attentive to the needs that you see. Find three people whom you can minister to today. It may be in your own family (your greatest place of ministry), in your church, on your job, or in your community. It may be a hug and an encouraging word to someone. It may be a material need that you can meet. It may be a message God wants you to share. That part will depend on your gifts, but friend, focus less on the gift and more on the Giver, and He will lead you moment by moment. That's real ministry!

Small Group Ideas

- Use these questions for discussion:
  - How can fear, insecurity, or social status keep someone from following God in ministry?
  - How can weakness and timidity be a hindrance to serving God?
  - What do you believe it means to be set apart for God?
  - How can someone overcome rejection to serve God?
  - Have you ever made a rash decision that you had to live with? What were the consequences?
  - Why do you think David was considered a man after God's own heart?
  - What do you think that really means?
  - Name some things that you believe keep women from serving God in ministry?
  - Name some things that are opportunities to minister that most people wouldn't think of.

- Look up and discuss the following Scriptures.
  - John 10:3, Matthew 4:19, Luke 9:23, John 12:26, Psalm 19:14, Psalm 37:4, Psalm 51:10, Psalm 86:11, Psalm 139:23, 2 Timothy 2:20-21

- You may want to play a song and have a time of quiet reflection at the end, encouraging ladies to commit to be used by God. We used the song "One Pure and Holy Passion" from the cd *Passion One Day Live*.[12]

Week 5

"Consider him who endured such opposition from sinful men, so that you will not grow weary and lose heart."

Hebrews 12:3

Faith and Opposition

Day 1—A Voice for God

Has God ever called you to confront someone in his sin?

I once was in a situation in which I was working for someone who was a Christian and in a position of ministry, but he was making decisions that were sinful and that would have repercussions, not only for him, but also for our workplace. I knew that those decisions came from a heart that really wanted what was best for the ministry, but they were wrong, nonetheless.

I prayed and prayed, and I did not want to be the one to discuss the situation with him, but I finally came to the conclusion that I would be disobedient if I didn't. And I really loved him. I didn't want to hurt him. I am sorry to say that he did not receive what I shared with him. It was a difficult time for me and for him. The ministry eventually closed, which hurt a lot of people. Needless to say, I don't like confrontation. But God sometimes calls us to it. We are not responsible for the results—only our obedience to share the truth in love.

Samuel was a man God called to speak for Him. And it often involved confrontation. Today we will wrap up Hebrews 11:32 with a study of Samuel. "And what more shall I say? I do not have time to tell about Gideon, Barak, Samson, Jephthah, David, Samuel and the prophets..."

His story is in the book of 1 Samuel, but again we will read parts and summarize parts. Let's begin with the story of his birth in 1 Samuel 1-3.

What promise did Hannah make to God if He would grant her a son?

Her promise was basically a vow to raise him as a Nazirite (set apart for God) just as Samson and John the Baptist were.

How old was Samuel when he was taken to live in the temple? What does 1:28 say that Samuel did when he got there?

Who was the priest? Who were his two sons?

Eli's two sons were wicked. So God raised up Samuel to serve Him as prophet. What happened to Eli and his two sons? Scan over chapter 4.

Samuel led Israel as judge and prophet. In chapter 7, he led Israel to victory over the Philistines. In chapter 8, the Israelites cried out for a king. God told Samuel to warn them of the dangers of having a human king, but to give them what they asked for. God called Saul to be the first king, and Samuel anointed him and gave him instructions for leadership.

> Samuel was faithful to speak for God and tell the people what God wanted him to say, even if the words were not pleasant. Let's read chapter 12:16-25. Despite their sin in rejecting God, what did Samuel encourage the people to do?

Now read chapter 15:1-23. Samuel was faithful to confront the king when he sinned against God, even though Saul could have had Samuel killed for doing so. We see in Samuel a man who was dedicated to the Lord all his life and who was faithful as a prophet to speak all that God told him to.

We, too, have the opportunity to be a faithful voice for God. We should seek God daily and when He speaks, we should listen. When God calls us to speak for Him, we must obey His voice.

"Brothers, if someone is caught in a sin, you who are spiritual should restore him gently. But watch yourself, or you also may be tempted. Carry each other's burdens, and in this way you will fulfill the law of Christ" (Galatians 6:1).

Of course, we must each test our own heart. Remember, the goal is not to judge or criticize; the goal is to help a brother or sister.

"Two are better than one, because they have a good return for their work: If one falls down, his friend can help him up. But pity the man who falls and has no one to help him up!" (Ecclesiastes 4:9-10).

At some point, we all need a Samuel to speak into our lives; let's be faithful to be a Samuel to someone else, if God calls us to.

The key to speaking for God is to allow God to speak to us. We must be spending time daily in His presence: reading and studying His Word, praying, and worshiping. We must learn how to listen and hear the voice of God.

"The man who enters by the gate is the shepherd of his sheep. The watchman opens the gate for him, and the sheep listen to his voice. He calls his own sheep by name and leads them out. When he has brought out all his own, he goes ahead of them, and his sheep follow him because they know his voice. But they will never follow a stranger; in fact, they will run away from him because they do not recognize a stranger's voice" (John 10:2-5).

"I am the good shepherd; I know my sheep and my sheep know me" (John 10:14).

Do you know His voice?

Day 2—A Bold Faith

You don't have to look at a news feed on social media for very long to see that a biblical worldview is quickly fading in America. Christians are seen as intolerant for believing in the biblical values that we hold dear. We are portrayed as hate mongers and bigots for taking a stand for biblical marriage, the right to life, or Christian education. Sometimes these names are deserved. "Christians" can certainly be mean.

Please don't misunderstand my intentions here. I realize that we need to take a strong stand for that in which we believe. But there is a right and wrong way to do anything.

As we tackle this week's topic on faith and opposition, we are going to see a different perspective from what we normally take on this issue. I pray that you will open your heart to receive this understanding. I realize that Christians will always face opposition because Satan is the enemy of God's people. I also believe we can learn from these Scriptures how to approach opposition in a way that will impact others with love and truth, rather than turning them further against Christ.

Today we are going to look at the next verse in Hebrews, which is a continuation of the last verse.

> And what more shall I say? I do not have time to tell about Gideon, Barak, Samson, Jephthah, David, Samuel and the prophets, who through faith conquered kingdoms, administered justice, and gained what was promised; who shut the mouths of lions, quenched the fury of the flames, and escaped the edge of the sword; whose weakness was turned to strength; and who became powerful in battle and routed foreign armies (Hebrews 11:32-34).

The last part of verse 33 reads, "who shut the mouths of lions." Daniel is not mentioned by name, but this verse refers to his ordeal with King Nebuchadnezzar in the lion's den. For his story, let's start with a brief history lesson.

So Israel started with Jacob and his twelve sons, the twelve tribes of Israel. Through Joseph they ended up in Egypt to escape famine. Through Moses and Joshua, they were led back to the Promised Land. The period of Judges began with Joshua and ended with Samuel. Samuel anointed Saul as king, initiating the period of the kings.

The kingdom remained united under Saul and David, but then was divided under the rule of David's son, Solomon, because he "did evil in the eyes of the Lord; he did not follow the Lord completely as David his father had done" (1 Kings 11:6). Solomon took many heathen wives who led him astray. But because God promised David that his throne would endure forever, Solomon's descendants remained on the throne of Judah, the southern tribe where Jerusalem was located. Other kings reigned over the northern portion, Israel.

Kings and prophets came and went for many years until we come to Daniel's story. Because of the Israelites' idolatry, God allowed them to be conquered by foreign empires. Israel fell to the Assyrians in 722 BC; Judah fell to the Babylonians in 586, and Jerusalem was destroyed. It was during this time that we find Daniel.

Let's begin by reading Daniel 1. What was different about Daniel and his three friends?

How did Daniel show his faith in God here in the very beginning?

Read chapter 2. How did Daniel show his faith, humility, and honesty?

Chapter 3 is about Daniel's three friends whom we will look at tomorrow. In chapter 4, Nebuchadnezzar had a dream that God again revealed to Daniel and he interpreted. By chapter 5, Nebuchadnezzar had died and Belshazzar was king. Daniel interpreted some writing that revealed God's judgment on the king and then he also died. By chapter 6, Darius was the king.

Read chapter 6. Why were the other administrators angry with Daniel?

Why did they want to get King Darius to make up a new law against praying to any god or king besides Darius?

What was Daniel's response to this new law?

What was Darius's response? Why?

According to verse 23, why was Daniel saved from the mouth of the lions?

I find something very interesting about Daniel and that is his wisdom. He was in a foreign land, under a hostile regime, and yet (like Joseph) he made himself valuable to the authorities. He respected those authorities without compromising his faith in God. He wouldn't compromise the dietary law, and he didn't fail to pray to God, even though it meant breaking the law. In verse 22, he declared to King Darius that he had never done wrong to him. In reality he hadn't, because the law was bogus and the king knew it.

God may one day allow us to live or work under conditions that may be hostile to us as Christians. How does He want us to respond? I believe that we should maintain our witness and be true to God's Word no matter what, but I also believe that we need to be careful about how we respond to authority. Daniel and his friends would have been killed in the very beginning if Daniel had not spent the night in prayer and then looked for a way to be valuable to the king.

Sometimes I think we get really "bold" in what we believe as Christians to the point of being antagonistic toward those who are lost. We may need to spend some time in prayer and ask God to show us how He would have us respond. We should not compromise on His Word, EVER! But we also need to use some wisdom and tact in how we respond to those who don't believe. Remember we are trying to win a lost world to Christ. The reason those in darkness live the way they do is that they have not seen the LIGHT!

Daniel helped those kings, and possibly others around him, to see that His God was the true God—not by being antagonistic, but through humility, honesty, and faith in His God.

We can help those around us who are lost and maybe even hostile towards us and our God by showing them the truth in love. Daniel was not a push-over! We don't see him being a wimp. He didn't compromise. But the foreign king liked him. Why? Maybe because he was humble and submissive and helpful. Maybe because he was honest. Maybe just because the favor of God was on him. I don't know. But I believe that if we will seek God, He will show us how to live in such a way that we can truly impact the world around us in a positive light without compromising our faith.

Daniel was credited with shutting the lions' mouths because He had faith in One who could. Daniel didn't shut the lions' mouth—Jesus did. He will do the same for you.

Day 3—A Simple Faith

Today we move on to the next verse which is a continuation of the two previous verses. The writer of Hebrews is telling us of many others whose faith is to be commended, such as those who "quenched the fury of the flames, and escaped the edge of the sword; whose weakness was turned to strength; and who became powerful in battle and routed foreign enemies" (Hebrews 11:34). This verse could be referring to many people whose stories are told in the Bible; however, they are not named. The first reference, though, seems to refer to Daniel's friends, Hananiah, Mishael, and Azariah. For their story, we turn back to Daniel chapter 3.

Remember that Daniel and his three friends were captives from Judah who ended up in Babylon under a foreign regime. We know about them that they, along with Daniel, refused to defile themselves with the king's food. We also know from Daniel 1:17 that God gave them knowledge and understanding.

One thing I would like to point out here is that they were given Babylonian names. Hananiah's Hebrew name means "the Lord shows grace," but his Babylonian name, Shadrach, means "command of Aku (Sumerian moon-god). Mishael's Hebrew name means "Who is what God is?" but his Babylonian name, Meschach, means "Who is what Aku is?" Azariah's Hebrew name means "the Lord helps," but his Babylonian name means "servant of Nabu."[13] These names were obviously given to show that the God of the Israelites had been replaced by the gods of the Babylonians. But in their hearts, this was not true. Although the Bible refers to them in chapter 3 by their Babylonian names, I want to refer to them by their Hebrew names. It just seems appropriate to do so.

Read Daniel 3. What had King Nebuchadnezzar made?

Historians believe that the image probably represented the god Nabu, from whom Nebuchadnezzar's name was derived. In Akkadian, "Nebuchadnezzar" means "Nabu, protect my son!"[14]

What did Nebuchadnezzar command everyone to do?

How did the three Hebrew boys respond?

When brought before Nebuchadnezzar, what did they say?

What happened to the soldiers that threw them into the furnace?

What happened to the three boys? (See verse 27)?

Who did Nebuchadnezzar see in the furnace?

What did he declare in verse 28?

Hananiah, Mishael, and Azariah showed great faith through their courage in the face of terrible suffering and death. They, like Daniel, were not willing to compromise their faith by worshiping a false god, which would have broken what two commandments?

Notice that when they were confronted by the king in verses 16-18, they did not try to defend themselves or explain the Ten Commandments. They didn't feel the need to try to persuade the king to understand their laws. They simply told the king that they believed their God would save them. But notice the second thing they told him: even if He does not, we still will not bow and worship the image or serve the false gods. They didn't attack the king or his law. They only stood firmly on the truth of God and His Word.

I believe that as Christians, we need to stop trying to defend ourselves or convince unbelievers why our way is right. Arguing with unbelievers is a lost cause—especially on social media! We need simply to *do* what is right and trust God with the outcome. What if instead of arguing against gay marriage, we just lived out our own marriages with love and grace? Wouldn't that be a great witness to the world!

That is the faith that convinces the lost that we are for real and our God is for real. Lost people will respect those who simply believe something and stick to it. Hananaiah, Mishael, and Azariah just believed God and followed His Word.

I'm not saying that we shouldn't speak out at all against the loss of values in our nation. We should always speak truth, just like those three Hebrew boys did. But remember: all they did was say what they refused to do. They didn't argue nor condemn those who bowed. They just refused to bow themselves. Even to the death.

When we respond to times of opposition with anger and hostility, we show the world the exact opposite of what Jesus told us to. I know how difficult it can be to feel attacked in our beliefs. We so want to defend our Lord and His Word. But let me assure you of one thing: Jesus can defend Himself.

And He does that best when we respond with His love and grace. Jesus did confront the religious leaders, but I fear sometimes that if He were still here in the flesh, He would be confronting us rather than the lost out there who oppose us!

So how do we deal with the multitude of attacks on our faith?

1. Pray for the other person.
2. Pray for wisdom in how to respond (or if you should).
3. Walk in love toward others.
4. Stand for what is right and biblical.
5. If you have to confront, do it in love.

The world needs to see the love of Jesus in us. The love of Jesus. In us.

Day 4—A Living Hope

The words we speak are so important; they have the power to bring life or death, light or darkness, hope or despair.

"The tongue has the power of life and death, and those who love it will eat its fruit," (Proverbs 18:21).

Sometimes opposition comes in the form of job loss, disappointments, sickness, death, or other circumstances beyond our control. Part of facing these situations with faith is guarding the words we choose to speak.

Today we will look at only the first part of Hebrews 11:35 - "Women received back their dead, raised to life again." This calls to mind two stories from the Old Testament—the widow of Zarephath in 1 Kings 17:7-24 and the Shunammite woman in 2 Kings 4:8-36.

Let's begin with 1 Kings 17:7-24. This story takes place during the time of Israel's division, when many different kings reigned and many prophets served. At this time Ahab was king of Israel, and he was an evil, wicked king. Elijah was the prophet for God. Because of the evil of the people, the Lord brought a drought and famine to the area.

Why did God send Elijah to the widow of Zarephath?

What was the widow planning to do?

What did God promise her?

When her son died, how did she respond to Elijah?

Whose faith brought the boy back to life?

Now read 2 Kings 4:8-36. Elijah had been a great prophet of God, and when he died, his follower, Elisha, received a double portion of his spirit. Why do you think the Shunammite woman invited Elisha to stay with them?

What did God do for her to repay her kindness for her hospitality to Elisha?

When her son died, what did she do?

When her husband asked why she was going to Elisha, what did she say?

When Gehazi asked what was wrong, what did she say?

Why do you believe she responded in this way?

She had faith in Elisha as a holy man, but whose faith brought the boy back to life?

Sometimes when God gives us a promise, it may seem that He turns around and takes it away. Both of these women questioned the prophets as to why God gave them sons, only to take them away. But both women acknowledged that the prophets were men of God and would speak the Word of God and help them with their situations.

We may sometimes be weak and feel that we don't have the faith to see God turn things around. Sometimes it seems that a dream has died or our hope seems dim. In these times, we need to acknowledge the Word of God as our only hope. These prophets were the Word of God for these two women, but we have the written Word of God.

It is in these seasons that we need to hold out the Word of God with the Holy Spirit as our guide and trust that God will come through. We have the Spirit to intercede for us when we don't know the words to say.

Read Romans 8:26 and copy it here:

These two women didn't know where to turn except to the prophets who spoke for God. We have only to turn to the Spirit of God and the Word of God to find hope.

Jesus brought us victory through His resurrection from the dead. Even when things seem hopeless, God can resurrect anything if we only believe. Even those things that seem already dead can be brought back to life.

"Praise be to the God and Father of our Lord Jesus Christ! In his great mercy he has given us new birth into a living hope through the resurrection of Jesus Christ from the dead..." (1 Peter 1:3).

Because our Savior has been raised, we are never without hope. The faith of these women was in the prophets, but the faith of these prophets was in our Lord. In whom is your faith?

Day 5—A Better Resurrection

The Body of Christ has recently witnessed the beheading of brothers and sisters for their faith. Such persecution calls to mind this section of Hebrews. In our look at faith and opposition today, we are going to study those who made the ultimate sacrifice for Jesus. I pray that none of us have our faith tested in this way; but should this test ever come, may we show ourselves faithful unto death.

Read Hebrews 11:34b-40. Name some of the things that were done to the people of God.

- _____
- _____
- _____
- _____
- _____
- _____
- _____
- _____

Why was it that even though some were tortured, they refused to be released?

These are prophets that would have had to recant the words they spoke for God in order to be released, so they refused. They knew God had a promise waiting for them, even though they never saw it fulfilled in this life.

None of the people are named in this section, but we know from history about the martyrdom of some.

- The prophet Zechariah, son of Jehoiada the priest, was stoned for speaking for God. Read 2 Chronicles 24:20-21.
- Jewish tradition holds that the prophet Jeremiah was stoned to death.
- Jewish tradition holds that the prophet Isaiah was sawed in two by the wicked king, Manassah.

- Read Nehemiah 9:26. Many prophets were killed for speaking the word of the Lord.
- Those who went around in sheepskins and goatskins and wandered in deserts and mountains could refer to John the Baptist, who was beheaded.

So what do all of these men have in common besides the fact that they were killed for their faith in God? Read Hebrews 11:39-40 again:

> "These were all commended for their faith, yet none of them received what had been promised. God had planned something better for us so that only together with us would they be made perfect."

You see, like Abraham, they were all looking ahead to a resurrection and a future home that had not yet been secured through Christ. The fulfillment of all that had been promised for those who believe happened when the perfect Son of God left the throne room of heaven and came to earth as a man. The promise was secured at Calvary.

They held on to the end because they believed the promise of what was to come. Their faith was in God and His promises. His promises were fulfilled through His Son, through whom they now have redemption along with us.

These men and women of faith had something that many around them did not. They were surrounded by people who did not believe in God and His promises. That's what set them apart from the rest. Look what Jesus had to say about many of the Israelites of His day. Remember, these were all part of the nation of the promise! Read Luke 11:37-54.

Many of the Israelites were not only opposed to, but hostile to the faith of these men of God, to the point that they killed some of them! Hebrews 11:38 says the world was not worthy of them, because they stood for what they believed even in the face of fierce opposition. Even without the promise being fulfilled!

How much more, then, should we—this side of the cross—be able to stand in the face of whatever opposition Satan brings our way? Jesus is the Lord of life! O death, where is your sting?

John 11:25-26 - "Jesus said to her, 'I am the resurrection and the life. He who believes in me will live, even though he dies, and whoever lives and believes in me will never die. Do you believe this?'"

Weekend Devo *Faith and Opposition*

So here we are at the end of week five. It's time to sit back and relax. Maybe have a cup of tea today. Let's reflect on this week's lessons about faith under fire.

We have learned this week about Samuel having the courage to speak for God, even when the message wasn't popular. We read about Daniel and his ability to stay true to his convictions in the face of opposition. We studied Shadrach, Meshach, and Abednego, who trusted God to defend them when their faith came under fire. We looked at two women who believed God's Word to turn things around for them. And we admired the many martyrs of the faith who never backed down from God's truth and never lost sight of the promise.

Wow! That's a lot of faith for you and me to measure up to! The good news is that we don't have to measure up to their level of faith, but just stay true to God where we are. So let's look at five lessons that we can learn and apply to our lives no matter what we are going through.

1. **We need to spend time daily with God so that He can speak to us**. I believe the fear in knowing what to say comes from not spending time with God. When we are in His presence daily—reading, praying, and listening to God—we will have a sense of peace in speaking what God has put in our hearts. Journaling will help us to articulate what God is saying to us and put His message into our own words before we share it with others.

2. **We must respond with love to those who oppose us while not compromising God's Word.** I realize how difficult that can be, especially when we feel that our faith has been attacked, but I believe that we need to just keep doing what God called us to do with love, joy, and peace. The world needs to see Christians who will love consistently even when it's hard and painful. We can take a stand for what is right without being unloving toward those who are wrong.

3. **We must stop trying to defend God**. He does not need us to defend Him or His Word. He just needs us to obey Him. The battle belongs to the Lord. He is more than able to defend Himself.

4. **We need to believe God to turn our situation around by praying and staying positive.** If we speak negative words over our situation, we will be defeated already. Quote Scriptures over your circumstance and believe that God is able.

5. **We must never back down from God's truth and never lose sight of the promise.** God is God. He is King of the universe. His Word is perfect; it is truth; it is eternal. If we follow hard after God and His eternal kingdom, we have nothing to fear. Death has lost its sting. Jesus has defeated sin, Satan, and death forever more!

I don't know what you may be facing in your life right now, but I am praying for you even as I write these words, that your faith may not fail.

> Application: Take some time today to think about any opposition you may be facing because of your faith. Pray for those who oppose you, knowing that your battle is not with them, but with the enemy of your soul. If you are not facing any opposition right

now, then take some time to pray for your pastor, spiritual leaders in your community, and leaders in our government who stand for God's truth. Ask God to prepare you for any opposition that may come to you, your family, or your church.

Small Group Ideas

- Use these questions for discussion.
    - Have you ever shared your faith with a lost person? What happened?
    - Have you ever missed an opportunity to share your faith with someone? What do you think held you back? What could you do differently next time?
    - Discuss some ways you can be a witness in your community.
    - How can we show love to those who don't agree with our beliefs without feeling as if we are condoning their sinful behavior?
    - What do you think impacts a lost person more—convincing them that they are wrong or loving them when they don't deserve it?
    - Why do you believe that Christianity grows under persecution?

- Have these Scriptures printed on index cards before the group session. On one side, print the heading; on the other side, print the Scripture. Depending on the size of your group, you can make more than one card with the same Scripture.

Courage	Wisdom	Trust	Hope	Vision
Deut. 31:6	Prov. 3:5-7	Rom. 8:37	Rom. 12:12	1 Chron. 29:11
Jos. 1:9	Prov. 1:5	2 Cor. 10:3-4	Rom. 15:13	2 Cor. 2:14
2 Chron. 32:7-8	James 1:5	Eph. 6:11	Eph. 1:18	Prov. 23:18
1 Cor. 15:58		James 4:7		

- Have the cards on a table with the heading side up. Ask each participant to prayerfully choose a card with the word that she feels she needs most in her life right now. Have her read the Scripture silently. You may wish to let each person pray for the person whose name they chose on the first day, asking God to give her more of what she needs in her life. Play some soft worship music in the background. Let this be a time for your group to minister to each other.
- Be especially sensitive to those who may be facing serious opposition in their lives. Pray for them, but refrain from giving advice. Ask God to give them comfort, strength, peace, and wisdom.

Week 6

"This is the victory that overcomes the world, even our faith."

1 John 5:4b

Faith and Victory

Day 1—A Great Cloud

Today, we come to the first of the three verses that are the focus of our study—Hebrews 12:1. It reads:

> "Therefore, since we are surrounded by such a great cloud of witnesses, let us throw off everything that hinders and the sin that so easily entangles, and let us run with perseverance the race marked out for us."

I love the word *therefore.* The whole point of our study up until today has been to understand the "therefore." The word *therefore* means "for that reason."[15] For what reason? The only way to fully appreciate what the writer of Hebrews is saying in this verse is to study "the reason." That's why we have spent the last five weeks studying all of chapter 11.

The reason is that "we are surrounded by such a great cloud of witnesses." I used to think this verse meant that all those people in chapter 11 are watching us and witnessing us in our "race." However, the word translated "witness" comes from the Greek word *martus* and is the origin of the English word *martyr.* In this verse the word *witnesses* means "testifiers" or witnesses to the truth.[16] They are not witnesses of our races, but witnesses and testifiers of their own races. These men and women today are in heaven with the Lord as witnesses of His great faithfulness. Their stories in the Bible testify to the power of their faith and the greatness of our God!

> Therefore, since we are surrounded (in the heavenly realm) by such a great cloud of witnesses (who testify of the power and faithfulness of our God), what ought we to do?

> We are to run with perseverance the raced marked out for us! Here the writer of Hebrews is using an analogy. Our Christian life is being compared to what?

Foot races can be traced back to the early Olympic races in Greece and Rome. The fastest and shortest race was called the stade race and was a distance of 200 yards, down the center of the stadium. In a two-stade race, the length was doubled. These increased all the way to the dolichos, which was twenty-four stades, or a distance of three miles.[17] There was no such thing as a marathon, so when the writer of Hebrews refers to running with perseverance, he probably had in mind the dolichos, because it was the longest race and would require endurance.

So how do we endure?

The verse tells us to "throw off everything that hinders." Using the analogy of a foot race, let's think of some of the hindrances that would keep one from making progress to the finish line.

Distractions:

Just as we can be distracted by things on the sidelines of a race, we can allow things in life to distract us. Name some things that are distractions to your spiritual growth, quiet time, etc.

What can you do to "throw off" these hindrances?

Other people:

In a race, we sometimes get competitive or look around at others in the race and feel inferior or superior. Do you let the attitudes, comments, or behaviors of others hinder you in your race? Read Galatians 5:6-7. Think about how your decisions might be influenced by others.

What can you do to "throw off" these hindrances?

Injuries:

Just as a physical injury can stop us in a race, pain from our past and hurt in our hearts can weigh us down and keep us from running our race. Think about the things in your life that cause you pain and keep you from going forward.

What can you do to "throw off" these hindrances?

Weather:

In a race, sometimes the weather does not cooperate and can slow us down. In life, sometimes we are faced with circumstances that, like the weather, are beyond our control. What are some circumstances in your life that are keeping you from making progress with God?

What can you do to "throw off" these hindrances?

Mental Attitude:

As a runner, one must be focused on the finish line and not allow thoughts that will discourage or impede his journey. As Christians, we must keep our focus on the Lord and not allow "stinking thinking" that will cloud our vision and slow our progress. What are some mental attitudes that may be slowing you down?

What can you do to "throw off" these hindrances?

All of the things that hinder may not necessarily be bad. They may be good or neutral things in our lives, but we just need to pay attention to them and throw aside those things that hinder our growth. We will look at the rest of this verse tomorrow. Please spend some time on this lesson today and allow the Lord to show you anything that is hindering your race.

Day 2—A Long Race

Yesterday we looked at the first part of Hebrews 12:1—"Therefore, since we are surrounded by such a great cloud of witnesses, let us throw off everything that hinders..."

Today, let's look at the next part of this verse: "and the sin that so easily entangles, and let us run with perseverance the race marked out for us." Of course, nobody likes to talk about sin, but the truth is that sin is what separates us from a holy God and keeps us, many times, from running our race as we should.

Imagine running in a race and all of a sudden you realize that your shoes have come untied—both of them! You don't want to stop because you are making good time and you don't want to deal with it. So you try to keep running and just sort of keep your eyes on the strings so you won't trip. But it seems as if the laces are getting longer and longer. They are beginning to get up under your feet and you can't stop them. Suddenly, the inevitable happens, and you feel yourself about to face-plant on the asphalt. You go down hard. And it hurts.

You will probably be thinking, "Why didn't I just stop and deal with the problem?" Now you are not only behind in the race, but also injured and probably embarrassed. Had you just stopped and tied your shoes, you would be moving along, making progress toward the finish line.

This is a very accurate analogy of what sin does in our lives when we don't deal with it. We all sin. If we are saved, then we have the Holy Spirit of God and the Word of God to convict us of our sin. The good news is that Jesus died on the cross to pay the penalty of our sin: past, present, and future. That forgiveness goes into effect when we confess it. But many times we don't deal with the sin in our lives.

Read the following Scriptures and jot down what you get from each:
- Psalm 32:1-5

- Psalm 66:18

- Proverbs 28:13

- Isaiah 59:1-2

- James 1:13-15

You see, sin separates us from God, and there are several consequences to not dealing with it. God doesn't hear our prayers for other blessings when we have unconfessed sin in our hearts. We will not prosper or grow in our walk. In other words, sin hampers our race. James said that sin gives birth to death. Just like in the analogy, we try to justify it to ourselves or ignore it, but it *easily entangles*! That's why we need to deal with it quickly. When we don't, we fall, and we fall hard.

The solution is so simple. Just like the runner who needs only to stop and tie his shoes, God has given us a way to deal with our sin. It's called confession.
Read 1 John 1:9 and copy it here:

To confess means to agree with God that our sin is wrong. David said in Psalm 51 that his sin was against God Himself. If we agree with God about our sin, then we are not only confessing, but repenting, which means to turn away from that sin. We stop whatever the sin is and turn and go in the opposite direction away from that sin. That is the only way to deal with sin in our lives. Otherwise, it is going to trip us up.

> Read 1 Corinthians 9:24-27. Paul talked about the strict training and discipline that goes into running a race. Nobody competing in the Olympics would compete without training and strict discipline. In the same way, we are running a race, and the prize is our heavenly reward. Paul said he made his body his slave; in other words, he didn't allow the flesh to rule him, but his spirit instead.

> Read Romans 8:5-9. Here Paul talked about the same thing—a mind controlled by the spirit and not the flesh—which requires discipline. We will never be perfect, but we should strive to please God in all that we do. That includes dealing with sin quickly and turning away from it. The Holy Spirit will help us if we try.

The last part of this verse says "and let us run with perseverance the race marked out for us." Solomon said in Ecclesiastes 9:22, "The race is not to the swift." Running our race is not about being fast. It's about being committed and not giving up.

> Read Galatians 6:7-9. We have to strive to please the Spirit and not the flesh. How do we do this? By cultivating a relationship with Jesus through time with Him in His Word,

in worship, and in prayer. The more time you spend with Jesus, the more you will want to please Him. You will find yourself confessing sin immediately and staying "in touch" with Him throughout the day. The discipline won't seem so hard, much like the Olympian who can spend hours in training because of her love for the game.

Running our race with perseverance is about staying close to Jesus and not turning aside to the right or the left. Since we are surrounded by such a great cloud of witnesses—from Abel to Zechariah—surely we can throw aside our sin and run.

Day 3—The Author and Finisher

Today we read Hebrews 12:2, which follows:

> "Let us fix our eyes on Jesus, the author and perfecter of our faith, who for the joy set before him endured the cross, scorning its shame, and sat down at the right hand of God."

A runner must keep his eyes on the finish line. He has a goal—to cross the line—and mentally, he must picture himself crossing that line and finishing the race well. Our eyes must be fixed on the One for Whom we run this race. We cannot begin to look aside to the right or the left.

> Read Matthew 14:22-31. What made Peter begin to sink?

When Peter took his eyes off Jesus and began to look around at his circumstances, he began to go down. The same is true for us. We need to stay focused on who Jesus is and his goal for our lives as seen in the Great Commission: "Therefore go and make disciples of all nations, baptizing them in the name of the Father and of the Son and of the Holy Spirit, and teaching them to obey everything I have commanded you" (Matthew 28:19-20a).

We also cannot keep looking back. Read Philippians 3:12-14. We are not yet made perfect, but we have to keep moving forward and growing in our relationship with Jesus. We can't keep looking back at past mistakes or living in the past. We have to keep our eyes on Jesus and press on!

He is the author and perfecter or finisher of our faith. Our faith had to begin with Him.

> Read Ephesians 2:8-10. How are we saved? By our own effort or by the finished work of Christ on the cross?

So who began the work in us?

He is the author of our faith.

Who continues the daily work in us?

Read Philippians 2:13. Yes, God is the One working in us from day to day according to His purpose for us.

Who is going to complete the work in us?

Read Philippians 1:6. God is faithful to complete what He started in us at salvation.

So since Jesus is the author and finisher of our faith, we had better keep our eyes focused on Him, not looking behind at the past or around at our circumstances, but focused on the One Who is at work in us.

What better example do we have than that of Jesus Himself, "who for the joy set before him endured the cross..."? He never took His eyes off the prize. The joy set before Him was not the cross.

Read Isaiah 53:10-12. The cross was what He endured to get to the joy—sitting down at the right hand of the Father, having done His will of achieving salvation for you and me.

What is the joy set before us?

We may have to endure some pain, suffering, trials, temptations, and burdens before we get to the joy. Read the following Scriptures and jot down something about each one.
- Luke 14:27

- Romans 8:18

- 2 Corinthians 4:17

- 1 Peter 4:13

- 1 Peter 5:10

The only way we can endure the pain of living in this fallen world is to follow the example of our Lord, who surely suffered more than we ever will. We must keep our eyes on what is to come—life forever with Jesus. He is the author and the finisher of our faith. His love is everlasting. His Word is eternal. Nothing in this world can compare to what He has in store for us.

The Author will finish our story: "And they lived happily ever after."

Day 4—Consider Him

Today we study the last Scripture in our passage for Bible study: Hebrews 12:3. "Consider him who endured such opposition from sinful men, so that you will not grow weary and give up."

Consider Him.
- Jesus.
- Who endured.
- Such opposition.
- From sinful men.

So, let's consider Jesus. Why are we running this race in the first place? For Jesus. What does this race require? Endurance. Why do we need endurance? There is opposition. From whom? Sinful men. Whom did Jesus come to save? Sinful men. You know, the ones who opposed Him.

So let's consider Jesus. Who opposed Him and how did He face opposition?

The opposition actually began before Jesus was old enough to face it Himself, when Herod wanted to kill Him. Then Jesus grew up and prepared to enter the ministry. The first thing He faced was the temptation by Satan in the wilderness—opposition to the ministry. How did Jesus handle it?

Read Matthew 4:1-11 for the answer.

Jesus responded with the Word of God. Let's look at the next opposition. Jesus began to preach, calling people to repentance, calling disciples to follow Him, teaching in the synagogues, healing every disease and sickness. He taught the truth about God and His Word—things such as loving our enemies, not judging, looking at what is in the heart rather than outward acts of righteousness. He taught on fasting and prayer and giving to those in need. And He began to make enemies.

We first see this in Matthew 8:34, when Jesus delivered a man from demons and sent the demons into a herd of pigs. The pigs drowned in a lake, causing someone to lose his source of wealth, and the people of the town asked Jesus to leave.

Next we see in Matthew 9:3 that when Jesus told a paralytic that his sins were forgiven, He was accused of blasphemy. Soon after, in Matthew 9:11, the Pharisees questioned the disciples about Jesus' eating with "sinners." The more good Jesus did, the more His enemies accused Him. Read Matthew 9:34. Now look at how Jesus responded in Matthew 9:35. Write here what Jesus did next: "Jesus went through all the towns and villages, _____."

He sent the disciples out in Matthew 10, telling them that they would face opposition, but to not be afraid. Read Matthew 10:23. Jesus told the disciples to just continue to do what He called them to do.

In Matthew 11:28-30, He promised rest for the weary. In Matthew 12, He was accused of breaking the Law to heal on the Sabbath. He tried to teach sinful men the truth about the purpose of God's Law, but they refused to listen and in 12:14, they plotted how they might kill Him. Jesus just continued to heal.

The Pharisees and teachers of the Law continued to plot against Jesus and try to trap Him into breaking the Law. They turned the people against Him. They were offended at the truth because it exposed their evil deeds.

Jesus continued to teach God's truth, such as Matthew 18, where we read that Jesus taught on humility, love, and forgiveness. Again in chapter 19, the Pharisees tried to test Him on the Laws regarding divorce, but Jesus just continued to speak God's truth.

Jesus knew what was to come—that He would eventually be handed over to be crucified. But on the night of His crucifixion, He took time to eat the Passover meal with His disciples. He had fixed His eyes on what was to come. When faced with great opposition, Jesus continued to speak God's truth, to love others, and to pray.

Our ultimate example of Jesus in the face of opposition, is the Son of God, hanging on a cross, praying, "Father, forgive them, for they do not know what they are doing" (Luke 23:34).

So what does it mean to endure?

JESUS NEVER GAVE UP! He could have called down angels to rescue Him. He could have changed His mind when faced with such suffering. In John 10:18, He said He laid down His life of His own accord. It was His choice to endure until the end.

Why do we need to consider His example? So we "will not grow weary and give up." The writer of Hebrews wants you to be encouraged. We will face hardship. We will face discipline from God; we will face opposition from the enemy; but don't grow weary and give up!

Sometimes we get so tired of trying to serve God in the face of opposition that we do quit. We may still be praying and reading God's Word, but we have given up on church or ministry, because it's just too hard. People can be so difficult—especially in the church! We can be so sincere and earnest and passionate about what we believe God has called us to do, and then face opposition and discouragement within the church! Beloved, Jesus is encouraging you to not give up.

Read Hebrews 10:24-25. God has a place for you in His kingdom on earth, and He needs you. If Jesus can do it, so can you! You may face opposition, but you can respond like Jesus did:

JUST KEEP DOING WHAT HE CALLED YOU TO DO! He just kept loving and teaching and healing and reaching, and He has called you and me to do the same.

There is no greater calling than to follow in His footsteps in ministry, whether it is a position in the church, raising a godly family, or witnessing on your job. We are all called to be His disciples and follow Him, no matter where those footsteps lead us.

So, come on! Get up, lace up, and get moving! We've got a finish line to reach!

Day 5—Let's Run!

"Therefore, since we are surrounded by such a great cloud of witnesses, let us throw off everything that hinders and the sin that so easily entangles, and let us run with perseverance the race marked out for us. Let us fix our eyes on Jesus, the author and perfecter of our faith, who for the joy set before him endured the cross, scorning its shame, and sat down at the right hand of the throne of God. Consider him who endured such opposition from sinful men, so that you will not grow weary and lose heart" (Hebrews 12:1-3).

> In our country today we are seeing fewer and fewer Christians who are active in church and in ministry. Many Christians have grown weary and lost heart. Why do you think that is the case?

> I think part of the problem is that we live by our expectations rather than reality. We expect everyone in church to be saved, and they're not. We expect everyone to act like a Christian should, and they don't. Do you ever feel that some people in church are mean-spirited? Have you been hurt in church before?

We also expect all churches to be successful and look perfect, like we see on TV. And that's just not reality. They probably have problems and opposition behind those closed doors, too. Take a look at Jesus' ministry. If all you see is His standing on a mountainside in a flowing white gown, smiling and sharing bread and fish with children; sitting in a circle with His disciples, laughing and teaching; and touching and healing lepers with love and compassion, then you've missed a lot.

See Jesus...
- Fighting Satan in the wilderness (Matthew 4:1-11)
- Teaching on adultery and hatred and pride (Matthew 5)
- Confronting religious leaders and their hypocrisy (Matthew 23)
- Leaving behind unrepentant cities (Matthew 11:20-24)
- Fleeing towns where His life was threatened (Matthew 12:14-15)

- Accused of being Satan (Matthew 12:24)
- Rising before daybreak to pray (Mark 1:35)
- Warning His disciples of evil men (Matthew 10)
- Accused of not paying taxes (Matthew 17:24)
- Settling arguments among His disciples (Matthew 20:20-28)
- Dealing with unbelief among the disciples (Matthew 17:14-23)
- Turning over tables in the temple (Matthew 21:12-17)
- Having His authority questioned (Matthew 21:23-27)
- Praying and sweating drops of blood (Luke 22:44)
- Betrayed by one of His own disciples (Matthew 26:14-16)
- Disowned by one of His closest friends (Matthew 26:69-75)
- Arrested by men with swords (Matthew 26:47)
- Falsely accused and tried (Matthew 26:57-67, 27:11-26)
- Beaten, ridiculed, and humiliated (Matthew 27:27-44)
- Hanging on a cross for the sins of the world (Matthew 27:45-54)

And you thought this race was hard!

This is why Jesus said to count the cost before deciding to follow Him. Following Jesus is not easy. We have to be willing to get our hands dirty; we have to be willing to sacrifice our pride; we have to be willing to be uncomfortable. And most of all, we have to stop living some religious fantasy about church and see the Body of Christ as Jesus did—broken but worthy of love.

The real work of ministry is difficult and not without pain, but the rewards are so worth it! There can be no greater reward than to lead another soul to Christ, to disciple others and teach them God's Word, or to be received one day by our Father and hear Him say, "Well done, good and faithful servant!" You see, Jesus had some awesome, rewarding moments.

See Jesus...
- Healing the sick (Matthew 4:23-25, 8:1-17)
- Setting people free from demons (Matthew 8:28-34)
- Blessing the children (Matthew 19:13-15)
- Turning water into wine (John 2:1-11)
- Being victorious over the devil (Matthew 4:1-11)
- Forgiving sins (Matthew 9:2, John 8:1-11, John 4:1-26)
- Encouraging His disciples (Matthew 10:1-42)
- Preaching the Good News of the Kingdom of God (Matthew 13)
- Feeding the multitudes (Matthew 14:13-21)
- Calming storms (Matthew 8:23-27)
- Walking on water (Matthew 14:22-36)
- Giving sight to the blind (Matthew 9:27-30)
- Raising the dead (John 11:1-44)
- Giving rest to the weary (Matthew 11:25-30)
- Rising early to pray to His Father (Mark 1:35)

- Teaching the truth about God's Word (Matthew 5-7)
- Sharing the Passover with his disciples (Matthew 26:17-35)
- Overcoming the world (John 16:25-33)
- Overcoming sin (1 Corinthians 15:57)
- Overcoming the devil (Colossians 2:15)
- Overcoming the grave (1 Timothy 1:10)
- Sitting at the right hand of His Father in victory! (Ephesians 1:18-23)

The rewards of leading others to Christ, discipling others, bringing healing and comfort to those in need, teaching God's truth, and sharing your faith with others, far outweighs the opposition we face in ministry, as long as our eyes are on Jesus. We have to throw off every hindrance and sin and keep running for Christ's sake. In the end, His opinion is the only one that counts.

Paul said, "I have fought the good fight, I have finished the race, I have kept the faith" (2 Timothy 4:7).

Our testimony may not be in how we started this race, but in how we finish it. Maybe, like me, you've struggled in your faith and stumbled along the course. Maybe your laces are untied and you need to deal with some sin in your life. Maybe you have let circumstances or other people slow you down or stop you in your tracks. I don't know where you are in your race, but I know that the Lord of all can get you up and get you going again.

You will never be more joyful, peaceful, or blessed than when you are running your race.

It's time to get back on track and run with all our hearts toward that finish line. There are lives in the balance and a Savior who is counting on you and me.

So let's run.

Weekend Devo Let's Run!

So, here we are at the end of six weeks of study! I pray that this time you and I have spent together with the Lord has been as impactful for you as it has for me. As I write these words, it has actually been 15 months since I started this journey to uncover the depths of faith and its impact on my walk with God. I can't begin to tell you how I have grown in these last months. But I do want to share one last story with you.

As I worked on this Bible study throughout the past year, several times I felt in my spirit that God wanted me to physically run a race. Now mind you, I don't run. I like to walk, but I am not a runner. But God began to impress this more and more in my spirit. So I found a cell phone app called "c25k" (Couch to 5K®)[18] and I found a 5k I wanted to try. I started training in October for the 5k in December.

Now, if you are a runner, you are going to laugh hysterically at the rest of my story, but here goes.

This cell phone app tells you when to walk and when to run, gradually increasing the time that you run each day so your body can get used to it. The first day I only had to jog for 60 seconds at a time, alternating with 90 seconds of walking for a total of 20 minutes. Will you believe me when I say that I thought I was going to pass out?

The only reason I kept running that first day was because I felt like I had made a vow to God to complete this. The next day that I trained, I began to hear God's voice telling me to keep going, to not give up, and that He would help me. The third day of training, I was praying the whole time, but I kept hearing God's voice telling me He wanted to teach me something.

Days later, I was still sticking to my training sessions, but it was getting harder and harder. By the third week, I had to run for 3 minutes at a time. I'm embarrassed to say this, but I cried a little bit. It was challenging for me. It hurt. It was late and dark some days by the time I got home, but I was so determined to finish what I believed God had started in me.

I remember one night in particular, that I got home late and it was already getting dark. We have a dirt road in front of our house, which was where I ran every day (featured on the front cover of this book). I was too afraid to run all the way to the end of the road (to the main highway), so I ran back and forth the whole time in front of our house. As I was running, I started feeling really good. I looked up, and the stars were coming out, the moon was starting to shine, and I really felt as if God were showing me the beauty of serving Him. I felt His presence in that moment.

And then God did a beautiful thing for me. I looked up and saw my husband sitting on the front steps of our house. He was watching over me because he knew I didn't like being out in the dark by myself. I heard God's voice telling me that as I ran this race for Him, my husband would be by my side.

Fast forward a few weeks, and this training was really getting tough! By the sixth week, I was running for 8 minutes at a time. Some days I felt that I could barely put one foot in front of the other. Some days I was in tears as I struggled to complete my training, but I felt compelled by the Lord to keep going. Trust me, nothing else could have made me do it!

But as I ran, God would whisper in my ears, "This pain, this struggle you are facing in the physical, is what many women are suffering emotionally and spiritually. I want you to feel this pain and know that you can endure when you have to. You can do all things through Me. You can persevere through whatever you face. I want you to tell them."

By December, I was able to run two miles without stopping. I started developing muscles in my legs that I didn't know I had! I already felt that I had achieved more than I ever dreamed, but I was still determined to finish the race. A 5k is 3.1 miles. I had never run more than 2.6, but I wanted more than anything to finish the race.

December 13 arrived –race day. My family went with me for moral support, but I was still so nervous about being in the race all alone. It was an evening race, so it was dark and I was in an unfamiliar location. Just before the race began, my husband, Kenneth, told me he was going to run with me. He is a physical education teacher, so running a 5k without training was nothing for him. (Not to mention that I run so slowly, he could basically walk while I ran.)

We started out the race, and I felt so good. Kenneth was with me. The Christmas lights were beautiful. The weather was perfectly cool but not too cold. My kids and my sister were waiting for me at the finish line. I felt great!

Then mile three came.

The last part of it was uphill. By this time, most of the real runners were long finished, so they moved us slow people to the sidewalk so traffic in the street could resume. The sidewalk was not well lit and had broken places that were easy to trip over. I wanted to just stop and give up. My lungs hurt and I literally felt that I could not go on. But I thought of this Bible study and I thought of you.

And I kept going.

You see, life is difficult. Ministry is difficult. Living for God is difficult.

But…

WE. CAN. DO. IT.

We can do whatever God calls us to do. We can finish the race.

It took me forty-five minutes, but I crossed that line. I didn't stop. I didn't give up. It was so freeing! That is the feeling God wanted me to have. He wanted me to know what it would feel like to endure until the end.

And He wanted me to share it with you.

I don't know where you are on your journey. You may even be out of the race right now. God wants you to know that He is with you. He will give you what you need every step of the way if you will trust Him. You don't have to start out sprinting. Just start. You will discover faith that you didn't know you had. And as you begin to walk in that faith, you will find the freedom to be all that He called you to be. After all, you are surrounded by a whole cloud of witnesses who've been there—Moses, Rahab, Samuel, David. They are crowded around that finish line cheering you on, "Come on! You can do it! Run! Run! Run!"

I know...you can't see them.

That's why they call it faith.

Small Group Ideas

- When we did this study at our church, we made this last night a special night of fellowship. The ladies brought some drinks and snacks. Our room was set up with round tables, so I printed some discussion questions on strips of paper and put them in mason jars that I had decorated with ribbon and numbered each jar one through five for the five tables. While the ladies ate, I had them draw a number (1-5) and sit at that table for the discussion. This was just to mix things up a bit and let God decide who sat at each table.
- After the food and fellowship, they sat at the appropriate table and we discussed the following Scriptures together:
  - Acts 20:24
  - 1 Corinthians 9:24
  - Proverbs 4:10-12
  - Isaiah 40:31

- Then we had table discussions using the questions in the mason jars:
  - If there were no obstacles, I would...
  - My calling/ministry in God's Kingdom is...
  - The hindrances to my race are...
  - The sin I struggle most with is...
  - The fear I struggle most with is...

- We closed with the song from earlier in the study "One Pure and Holy Passion" and prayer.
- I pray these ideas will inspire you to develop some creative ideas of your own.

I would love to hear from you! If you enjoyed this Bible study/devotional or perhaps have some small group ideas to share, please contact me by email at deuter3312@yahoo.com.

New Life!

Do you want to know how to have new life?

We were each created by God to know and worship Him. God loves you and desires a personal relationship with you.

The Bible teaches us that we are all sinners. Romans 3:23 says, "for all have sinned and fall short of the glory of God." God is holy and righteous and good. He created the world and all that is in it. But we are all born with a sinful nature because He made us with a free will—the opportunity to choose whether or not we will follow Him. Left to ourselves, we will fall short of His glory and righteousness. This sin separates us from God and leads only to death. Romans 6:23 says, "for the wages of sin is death."

But because God loves us so much, He made a way for us to know Him through His Son. "But God demonstrates his own love for us in this: while we were still sinners, Christ died for us" (Romans 5:8). God sent His only Son, Jesus, who lived a perfect life, to die on the cross for us as payment for our sin. He took the punishment on Himself so that we could be free from sin's penalty.

The rest of Romans 6:23 (above) says this: "but the gift of God is eternal life in Christ Jesus." We are sinners, and yet through Jesus and the gift of God, we can have eternal life. The truth is that we really can have a personal relationship with God through His Son, Jesus.

So what do you do to be saved?

Romans 10:9-10 tells us "That if you confess with your mouth, 'Jesus is Lord,' and believe in your heart that God raised him from the dead, you will be saved. For it is with your heart that you believe and are justified, and it is with your mouth that you confess and are saved."

If God is speaking to your heart right now and you want to be saved, pray a prayer like this one:

> Lord God,
> I believe that You are God and that You created me to know You. I believe that
> You sent your Son to die on the cross for my sins and that He rose again and lives

forever. I know that I am a sinner and I confess my sins to You now. I ask You to forgive me and cleanse me and come to live inside my heart and be the Lord of my life. I choose to follow You and live for You from this day forward.
In Jesus' name,
Amen

If you just prayed a prayer like this one, please let me know the good news. Find a Bible-believing Christian church and begin to read the Bible and talk to God every day. You've just begun your new life in Him. Congratulations! Your life will never be the same!

Acknowledgments

I would like to thank those in my life whose prayers, sacrifices, support, encouragement, and participation have cheered me on in this leg of my race.

Kenneth, Josiah, and Bethany, your love and support mean the world to me. I couldn't write one word without you.

Mema, your advice, correction, and encouragement helped to shape this study. I love you more than words can say.

My students at Jesus Is Lord Christian School, you were the inspiration. Thank you for listening to my rambling about Jesus.

My family at Salem Baptist Church, you have been such a blessing to me and my family. Thanks, especially, to those ladies who walked through this study with me. You were the inspiration for the weekly devotionals and small group ideas.

John and Lillian Moore, your support made this book possible. Thank you for your generosity and obedience to God.

Tessa Stanton and Queen Harris, I am honored to minister alongside you. Thank you for the prayers and encouragement to run this race.

Grandma Mildred (in heaven), thank you for passing on your love for Jesus, for speaking, and for writing. I miss you!

There are many more of you—too many to name—who have helped me along this journey. I pray that God will richly bless you as you have blessed me.

And Jesus, it's all about You. To You be all the glory.

About the Author

Jennifer Hayes Yates is a Christian high school teacher, church music director, and speaker at women's events. She has studied and taught the Word of God for over 20 years. Jennifer has a passion for the Word, worship, and encouraging women to seek Jesus in an intimate relationship that will impact their world for Him. She and her husband Kenneth and their two children, Josiah and Bethany, make their home in Bennettsville, South Carolina. You can follow Jennifer on Twitter, Facebook, or blog at jenniferhyates.wordpress.com.

End Notes

1   Kenneth Barker, *The NIV Study Bible* (Grand Rapids, MI: Zondervan, 1984), 121.
2   William C. Martin, *The Layman's Bible Encyclopedia* (Nashville, TN: The Southwestern Company, 1964), 255.
3   Barker, *NIV Study Bible*, 14.
4   Charles F. Pfeiffer, *The Wycliffe Bible Commentary* (Nashville, TN: The Southwestern Company, 1962), 16.
5   Barker, *NIV Study Bible*, 1872.
6   Gary Smalley and John Trent, Ph.D, *Giving the Blessing* (Nashville, TN: Thomas Nelson Publishers, 1993).
7   Barker, *NIV Study Bible*, 42.
8   Ibid., 43.
9   Ibid., 46.
10 Ibid., 350.
11 *Strong's Exhaustive Concordance*. Available from the internet: Biblehub.com/greek/1248.htm
12 Nathan Nockels and Tom Laune, *Passion One Day Live* (Sparrow Records, 2000).
13 Barker, *NIV Study Bible*, 1300.
14 Ibid., 1303.
15 New Oxford American Dictionary (New York: Oxford University Press, online version, 2015), s.v. "therefore."
16 Barker, *NIV Study Bible*, 1874.
17 *Ancient Greek Thesaurus*, [online], available from the internet: www.greek-thesaurus.gr/olympia-sports-races.html
18 Josh Clark, www.c25k.com

Printed in the United States
By Bookmasters